Content copyright © Ogilvie R

Published by Ogilvie Ross LLP
15 Springfield Park
Kinross
KY13 8QS
www.ogilvieross.co.uk
info@ogilvieross.co.uk

Contents

Introduction

Negotiations take place in our personal and business lives on a daily basis, and sometimes we don't realise we are in a negotiation.

Great negotiators not only recognise when they are negotiating, but also know how to get the best possible deal out of the situation in which they find themselves. They often come across as being a very confident and completely credible individual who is in complete control regardless of the situation.

Unfortunately, this is not always the case for the rest of us.

This book aims to provide you with an understanding of the tools, techniques and strategies that will allow you to become a better negotiator.

Two Red Lines and a Toy Box?

Before I move on, I should probably provide a short explanation of the title, Two Red Lines and a Toy Box. For me, these are two of the most important concepts for any negotiator.

The Red Line is simply a boundary or limit, beyond which any agreement will not work. There are red lines everywhere in our lives, from the time that the gate closes for our flight, to the expiry date on our fresh milk or from the amount of money we have available for our holiday. It extends to the way we want to be treated in our personal and professional relationships. If any of these red lines are overstepped, then we know the impact-- we miss our flight or our coffee tastes foul; we could end up in debt or our relationship breaks down.

The Toy Box is a simply a container for the items you have available to play with in the negotiation. If I remember back to my daughter, who is now in her 20s and will be delighted to read this, and the performances she used to put on for us and our guests, she would go to her toy box and select the items that would support what she was trying to do. Rarely did she wear her dinosaur costume when playing a princess but when she did, it caused great confusion for the audience (and a little amusement). If we choose the wrong items to use in our negotiation then, no matter how good the performance, we are setting ourselves up to fail.

Your Journey

Before we broach the topic of negotiation, it is worth looking at the four stages[1] that you may well pass through on your journey to becoming a better negotiator. They are:

- Unconscious Inability
- Conscious Inability
- Conscious Ability
- Unconscious Ability

Think about getting to and from work, a favourite restaurant or your gym. Before you knew where you had to go, you had an *unconscious inability* to get there. You didn't know that you needed directions to get there, and it was not really a problem. Then, when you discovered that you had to be somewhere, you looked it up on a map and followed the detailed instructions to get there. You now have a *conscious inability* to get there. In other words, without the map, you would be completely lost and would struggle to find your destination. The next few times you travel to that location, you start to become less dependent on the map, perhaps only referring to it for the tricky junction or interchange. You are now moving into the *conscious ability* stage, where you

---

[1] *Adapted from "Four Stages for Learning Any New Skill" - Gordon Training International.*

still must concentrate to get to your destination, but it is getting easier. Finally, after a period of time, which can be different for each of us, you can get to your destination without really having to think at all. You can talk on the phone, listen to music and become lost in your thoughts without any concerns around finding the destination. You have now developed an *unconscious ability* to get to where you want to go.

If we now relate this to negotiating and assume that negotiating is a completely new skill for you then you have an *Unconscious Inability* to negotiate. At this stage, there is no recognition or understanding that you do not know how to negotiate as you have never tried to negotiate.

Once you try negotiating, you will develop a *Conscious Inability* to negotiate. Here you recognise the value of negotiating, but you still do not know how to do it properly, and – as a result – you will make mistakes from which you will, hopefully, learn as you progress through this stage.

Next you will develop a *Conscious Ability*, where you now understand how to negotiate but need to be constantly thinking and concentrating through all parts of the negotiation.

Finally, after a period of time, you will have an *Unconscious Ability* to negotiate. Here the skill will have become second nature and can be performed at will; some might think of it as being on autopilot. Be wary of this mindset. Do not go into any negotiation on autopilot. If anything, you should rely on your *Conscious Ability* to negotiate with a plan for every move.

Before we move on, take a look at the following section and spend a few minutes thinking about where you are in your journey to becoming a better negotiator.

Where Are You Now?

When asked questions that are intended to help us self-assess where we are in terms of skill proficiency, one of the challenges is to identify what the self-assessment is based on.

With this in mind and before you answer the questions on the next page, think about someone who you consider to be a good negotiator. This person would be a 10. When considering how you would rate yourself when answering the self-assessment questions, in your mind, imagine this person as a 10 and decide where you would be with that as your scale. If you cannot think of anybody then think about how you would describe a good negotiator. Use this as a 10.

Self-Assessment Questions

1. On a scale of 1 to 10 how would you rate...
    a. your ability to plan and prepare for a negotiation?
    b. your ability to get the outcome you are looking for?
    c. your ability to understand the counterparty and respond or react to their behaviour?

2. What would you consider you are good at when it comes to negotiating?

3. What would you consider you could be better at when it comes to negotiating?

4. Who are the most difficult people for you to negotiate with?

5. If you could improve one thing about your negotiations, what would that be?

Key Takeaways

Great negotiators:

- recognise when they are negotiating.
- know how to get the best possible deal.
- identify their Red Lines.
- know what to use from their Toy Box.
- plan and prepare for every situation relying on their *Conscious Ability* to get to where they need to.

Further Thought

Sometimes it can be good to reflect on those you consider to be good negotiators. Look at those within your team or organisation, but also look outside of your organisation and if you can, outside your industry. What do these individuals do well and what can we learn from them?

First Things First

What is a Negotiation?

When I ask this question, I get a range of answers such as...

"A process by which two or more parties come to a mutually beneficial agreement"

"A meeting between multiple parties where compromises are made to reach an agreement"

"A discussion that I lead, and I win"

For me, the answer is more general and wider ranging:

A negotiation is "a discussion that is intended to produce an agreement."

We will look at the process and steps required to get into a position where reaching an agreement becomes possible; however, before we move on, I want to look at the phrase "*intended to*" from my definition.

You should always go into a negotiation fully prepared and with the *intention* of reaching an agreement – even if you think there is little or no chance of achieving one because so much can change during the process. But you should be aware that sometimes you will have to walk away from a negotiation without an agreement because to reach an agreement under the current conditions would be detrimental to you personally, to your business or to the relationship between you and your counterparty. In other words, it goes beyond your red line.

Ultimately, you should always start any negotiation with a goal or objective in mind, but remember that the other parties involved in the negotiation are also interested in achieving their own goals objectives. This means you may be faced with a conflict of interests and goals, which can come from two sources:

- There is conflict between your own objectives. This just comes down to poor planning and can be easily fixed by following the planning process outlined in this book.
- There is conflict between your objectives and the objectives of the other parties in the negotiation. This is one of the fundamental starting points for a negotiation. If, after a discussion, you discover that there is no conflict, then you have an agreement right away, so there is no need to negotiate.

What Do You Need Before Negotiating?

If we look back at our definition of a negotiation (a discussion that is intended to produce an agreement), we can immediately pick out two things required before you consider negotiating, as well as a third that may not be quite as obvious:

1. Two or more parties
2. Something to discuss
3. A red line

Two or More Parties

If we accept that at a very basic level, a discussion is just a form of communication and that the basic definition of a communication is the transmission of information between a transmitter and a receiver, and that these are two different entities, then it is fair to say that you need to have two or more parties for a negotiation.

Unfortunately, many people will have already negotiated against themselves before they even meet the counterparty.

I was brought in to work with one organisation who wanted to increase their profitability. They were selling a range of products into the construction industry and had identified a price for their products that was at the upper end of their acceptable range and, if achieved, would bring a good profit. When I started the engagement, I discovered that the actual price being achieved was significantly below their target price and when I looked deeper, the initial price quoted was also, often, below this target price. When asked why, the over-arching response from the sales team was that they felt the target price was too high, especially as they knew others were charging less. They had fallen into the trap of negotiating with themselves before they had discussed anything with their customers. The good news is that with a little help, they changed their approach, became better at hitting their targets and added 3% to their bottom line.

So, just like the sales team above, how do you know that you are not going to get what you are looking for without asking your counterparty? I am not suggesting you wing it; you need to be robust during planning and believe in what you are looking for– just don't fall into the trap of negotiating against yourself.

Something to Discuss
The topic or topics for discussion can be loosely grouped into one of three headings:

- A disagreement
- A difference
- An overlap

With all three, it is often a case of opening our toy box and looking at what we have to play with in order to reach an agreement.

A Disagreement

If you view the definition of a disagreement as being a lack of agreement, a disparity, a conflict or a quarrel, then you can see that this is something that could be difficult to overcome. Sometimes disagreement results in arguments that become heated and emotional, and this can drive both parties further apart.

If you can take the emotion out of a disagreement, then it could simply be described as a "gap" between the parties that we need to bridge to get agreement.

A Difference

Sometimes there is just a difference of opinion or a misunderstanding that needs to be addressed before moving on. This will often manifest itself as a disagreement, but after further discussion, it may become clear that there is just a difference that needs to be explained.

An Overlap

An overlap is a type of negotiation that is overlooked as most people view a negotiation as trying to bring two or more parties together. Sometimes, both parties are together, but they are too blinkered to realise it. This can come about because the parties are not prepared share information, either because of a lack of trust, they believe that sharing information is dangerous in a negotiation, or they have been burnt in the past.

As part of our negotiation training programmes, we use simulations to reinforce learning and demonstrate key principles and with one of these simulations, there is complete overlap with the requirements of both parties. This simulation is typically used towards the end of the day, when both parties are tired, and the result is often reached long after it should have been. The reason is because both parties believe that the information they have on their instructions is in some way secret and should not be shared. When we debrief and share the instructions, there is a realisation that if they had simply said, "I have a problem that I hope you can help with and it is...", both parties would have found common ground very quickly.

Going into the negotiation with an open mind and not assuming that it will be a battle can help you recognise overlap.

A Red Line
This is the point beyond which you cannot or will not go. It is your walk-away point. It is the deal-breaking point. It needs to be firm and rational (not loose and emotional), otherwise it becomes very difficult to know when to stop and walk away from an unfavourable deal.

For example, let's say you are looking to buy the car of your dream; it doesn't matter if it is brand new or second hand, and you have decided that you don't really want to spend more than £10,000 on this car despite having £20,000 available. One day you spot an advert for this perfect car. The advertised price is £12,995 but regardless, you make an appointment and take it for a test-drive. Upon returning to the seller, you decide to hide the fact that it is even better than you had hoped and negotiate hard. After 60 minutes of intense discussion you have driven the seller down from £12,995 to £10,125, and they have told you that if you try to get one more penny off the price, they will walk away. You only need an additional £125, remember you had £10,000 spare, so, do you take the deal or walk away from the perfect car?

Over the years, I have used this same example to audiences from around the world and around 99% of those asked say the same thing: take the deal.

Why do so many people take the deal? After all this is a hypothetical situation and some who take the deal, don't even drive a car. I believe it is down to two reasons, emotion and scale.

If we look at scale, in the grand scheme of things, £125 is such a small number. It is only 1.25% of the £10,000 red line that was set, and so it is very easy to convince ourselves that is it OK to pay that little bit more. But why should the seller get the 1.25%? What difference would an additional 1.25% onto your bottom line make?

On the emotional side, it is the perfect car, and so there is an emotional bond created. That bond is very difficult to break, but not impossible. In the real world, emotion out ranks scale and that can cause us to spend the next six months justifying to everybody why it was the right decision.

When you are setting your red line, make sure it is achievable and if you need to, take account of your emotions. If there are others involved in the decision-making process or to whom you will have to report the outcome, make sure they also agree with and buy into your red line.

We have focussed on your red line here but remember that red lines exist for all parties in the negotiation and a knowledge or understanding of them can greatly strengthen your position in any negotiation.

Finally, remember that unless things have changed, any deal that is worse than your red line can result in a poor deal for you and needs to be rejected before you re-evaluate.

How Can You Reach Agreement?

There are two commonly accepted approaches you can take to try to solve the disagreement, settle the difference or cement the overlap:

1. The Positional approach
2. The Interests-based approach

The Positional Approach

This approach, also known as the Distributive or Competitive Approach, involves holding onto a fixed idea or position about what you want, and reasoning or arguing for it and it alone, regardless of any underlying interests.

A classic example of this is haggling in a market where a customer has a maximum amount they will pay and the stallholder has a minimum amount they will accept.

For example, you may recognise this scenario:

Customer: "How much is that rug?"

Market Trader: "Thirty dollars."

Customer: "How much? I'll give you ten."

Market Trader: "That is far too low. I will accept twenty-five."

Customer: "Fifteen, and not a penny more."

Market Trader: "The lowest I am prepared to accept is twenty."

Customer: "OK 20 it is."

The result of this is that the customer pays $10 more than they wanted, and the Market Trader gets $10 less than they wanted. Potentially not a great deal for either side but one that is acceptable.

The example above illustrates the back and forward nature of positional-based negotiations, and the more extreme the opening positions, the longer it will take to conclude the negotiation.

This is very often the first approach adopted in a negotiation and can become problematic because as the negotiation moves forward, the parties involved can become more and more entrenched. As a result, any agreement reached is often the result of mechanics – for example, splitting the difference.

Positional-based negotiation is less likely to result in a win-win outcome, as one side may not be happy with the result. It may also result in a breakdown in the relationship between the parties because of the "you" vs "me" approach.

Having said all that, there may well be times when this is the best approach to take – for example, you have terms of business that you really do not want to operate without, you will take a strong position and defend them. Payment terms is an example of this for one of my clients. They work very hard to maintain 120-days payment terms because of the nature of their business. Without these, there is a risk of impacting negatively on their cash flow, and while they can accept shorter periods, they take a very strong stance. Any variation comes at a cost for the other party.

This approach can be summarised by the following characteristics:

- Each side takes up a position, sometime without logic or rational, and defends it, initially through calm explanation which can then progress to irrational behaviour, stubbornness, anger, repetition or silence.
- Initial positions are often set at overly ambitious or unrealistic points, way beyond the estimated red line of the counterparty. This can be a deliberate tactic that is used to make any movement seem generous. Think about anytime you have tried to buy something in a culture where bartering is the norm. The initial quoted price can be up to 90% higher than the truly acceptable price.
- Any movement from the initial position will be small and will often be supported with a realistic sounding explanation such as, "I hear

what you are saying, but the current market conditions do not allow for such movements. The best I can do is 1%."

- Tactics such as emotions or expertise or relationship are used to gain short-term advantage. For example, they may say something along the lines of "I played golf with your boss at the weekend and they were saying how key this deal was to their strategy going forward" or "I am not sure why you think that will work. I have a team of experts who all tell me differently."

- There can be an overuse of "trust me" type of language such as "Honestly, this really is my best price" or "Trust me, I know what I am talking about, and you won't find this anywhere else."

- Information is withheld or misrepresented. For example, you may agree to a price or fee thinking that everything is included in it, but then further down the line, discover that the management fee or delivery or tax or expenses or spurious factors depending on the day of the week were not included.

- The outcome can often be a win-lose or lose-lose where one or both parties walk away with a deal that is less than satisfactory.

- The approach and tone of the counterparty is often more harsh or aggressive, and they may use tactics such as keeping you waiting or not turning up, intimidation through shouting or use of language or banging the table, bringing an extended team with them.

- There is no real interest in building long-term relationships, despite what may be said right at the very start.

- The conversation will often start with a position rather than a discussion around each other's interests, needs and possible alternatives. For example, "Hello and thank you for coming in. Before we start I should tell you that we will only pay £250 for that widget." Or "Good morning, we have two weeks to complete this and there is no scope to extend."

Dealing with the Positional Approach

If you think you have identified one or more of the above characteristics, then you should start to prepare for what could be a long and drawn out process.

Firstly, prepare yourself to absorb the pressure that they are going to try to apply, and if you are not someone who deals well with conflict, take a break and come back in with someone who does. If that is not an option, then do not be forced into making a decision there and then. Tell them you will take it all away and get back to them. This can also be a useful tactic as it can flush out true positions, especially if there are pressures on their side and they really need the deal.

Ask questions that are intended to show you are interested in them and their needs.

Look at your red lines; do you have any around commercial relationships? For example, if you have a red line that you are looking for a partnership-based commercial relationship, and they are showing no intention of working towards this, then trust your planning and the fact that walking away from the negotiation is acceptable, and tell them. Don't be intimidated into changing your red line.

If they start with an initial position that is extreme, then dismiss it immediately, both from the table and from your mind. Tell them that before you can even start to look at their offer, you have a number of questions you need answered. Then take control by using the questions to direct the conversation and start to frame *your* initial position.

If they are aggressive, don't be aggressive back. Fighting fire with fire may work sometimes, but there is a real risk that it will just make the fire bigger. Test the reality behind their anger by asking about it, not superficially but in detail. Tell them that you really want to fully understand the cause and what could be done to fix it. Sometimes this can be enough to turn the approach around completely into one that is much more interests based.

The Interests Approach

This approach, also known as the Integrative or Cooperative Approach, involves both parties collaborating to find a "win-win" solution. The focus is on developing mutually beneficial agreements based on the interests of all parties. Interests include the needs, desires, concerns and fears that are important to each side. These interests are often the hidden reasons behind the negotiation.

Basing your negotiation around interests often produces a more satisfactory result because the negative feelings and the final outcomes associated with the Positional Approach often do not really satisfy the true interests and needs of all parties.

Interests-based negotiations can also require a degree of creativity – trying to invent options for mutual gain that can potentially give all parties what they want. As soon as I mention the word creativity or ask clients to get creative, some come up with very creative options but for others, often the majority, I get some looks that range from fear to disbelief as they do not consider themselves to be creative in any way. For some in this category, it is because they consider creativity to be arty, and in their mind, the extent of their creativity is that they can just about draw stick figures. For others, it is because they are worried about stepping outside of the norm. This fear or concern can do more damage than good and can result in a poor or even failed negotiation. If you are at all concerned about becoming creative, get other colleagues involved. Involve people from other business areas as they will not have been as close to the negotiation as you and may well be able to offer solutions or challenge and develop your ideas.

There are often many interests behind any one position, and if all the parties involved identify and understand those interests, they will increase their ability to develop a favoured win-win solution.

A well-known example of this interests-based approach can be found in the Orange Dispute.

In the Orange Dispute, there is just one orange that needs to be used by both parties. The position is that both sides need the orange, and often the result is that the orange gets cut in half, as the feeling is that half an orange is better than no orange. But if one party were to take a moment and ask one simple question, they may be able to find a much better solution...

For example:

A brother and a sister walk into the kitchen and see that there is just one orange left in the fruit bowl.

Brother: "I need that orange."

Sister: "So do I!"

Brother: "Well I need it more than you and I am going to take it."

Sister: "Oh no you are not. I need it more than you, so I am taking it!"

I am sure, at this point, some of you are substituting something else for the orange and are also able to recognise that this is an example of the Positional Approach in action.

In this case, there is usually a call for a mediator, mum or dad, which may result in the orange being divided between the two siblings as the mediator just wants a quiet life. But what if the sister tried the following...?

Sister: "Why do you need the orange?"

Brother: "Because I am baking a cake and need to grate the skin into the mixture."

Sister: "OK, well, I just wanted to make a glass of freshly squeezed orange juice, so why don't you grate the skin and then give me the rest of the orange to make my drink?"

Everybody wins! The two siblings get what they wanted; there is no fighting, screaming and crying and mum and dad are not needed.

Even though this is a very simple example, the solutions reached through an Interests Approach are often much more satisfying to everyone involved and can have the additional benefit of creating long-lasting, positive relationships, even between parties who have previously been in conflict.

The other benefit which is often overlooked, is establishing a trend for a chosen approach for the next negotiation. There is more chance that the next time the two counterparties meet, they will try to find a solution to the problem that does not start with demands but starts with dialogue.

There is also an increased chance that the next time either counterparty is involved in a negotiation, they will start off with the Interests Approach.

This approach can be summarised by the following characteristics:

- There is an open acknowledgement that all sides have needs and feelings and will be given time and space to discuss them. Questions such as "Tell me more about?" or "What are you looking for?" are not just asked, the answers are sincerely listened to.

- Fair and reasonable alternatives or solutions are developed during the discussions.
- Trust is built based on mutual respect on both an organisational and personal level. Personal credibility is not attacked, even when mistakes are made.
- Information is openly shared with all parties being prepared to be open and honest with their answers to questions.
- There is a willingness from both parties to trade concessions to try to reach agreement.
- Behaviour that is unacceptable is addressed.
- Alternatives are openly explored through phrases such as "Would an additional month be beneficial?" or "It would be great if we could fix that at 1% for the next 6 months and then review it".

The usual outcome of the Interests Approach is win-win with both parties feeling satisfied with the outcome. As Napoleon said, "The objective of negotiation should not be a dead opponent."

To make this approach work, you must put interests at the centre of the negotiation. Each party should attempt to understand their own and others' needs and take steps to fulfil them.

To identify interests, you may want to:

- Consider the six human needs:

- o Certainty – how can we provide a degree of comfort that what we say will happen will happen?
- o Variety – what can we do to ensure that we don't get stuck in a rut?
- o Significance – how can we make them feel like a true partner in the process rather than an opponent?
- o Contribution – what do we need to do to ensure that they feel they have not only contributed but have also added to the situation?
- o Love – how can we make them want to take part and look forward to the next meeting with anticipation?
- o Growth – what can we do to help them feel that they have personally benefitted from the negotiation, in more than just a financial way?
- Ask open questions to create dialogue.
- Ask "Why?" and "Why not?" questions.
- Identify shared interests and build on them.
- Identify multiple interests that support the problem.
- Acknowledge the counterparty's needs and interests as part of the process.
- Adopt a positive attitude towards addressing the opportunity rather than adopting a

negative problem based on the attitude during the negotiation.

Several years ago, I was brought in to work with a national government during the merging of eight distinct organisations who all provided the same public service into one centrally controlled organisation. At the same time, they were trying to bring in a new governance organisation. The overarching style of both parties could have been described as "I want to be in control and I don't care what they think because I am right!" Needless to say, this caused problems and most of the pre-merger meetings were very difficult, very acrimonious and made very little progress. We introduced a process of starting each meeting by letting each party outline the high-level areas that they wanted to discuss and then talking through them one at a time, without interruption or dissent. It was difficult to start off with, but as time went by and each party actually listened to what was being said, they started to realise that there was common ground they could build on, and they started to become more open, make progress and reach small but important agreements. They started to build on interests rather than positions. Ultimately the merger was completed, and the governance structures put in place, but it was and continues to be a difficult situation which requires patience and understanding from all involved.

A Third Approach

At this point, I should probably point out a third approach that can be used to bridge a gap, and that is to use a third party – essentially mediation or arbitration. As the focus of this course is negotiation rather than mediation or arbitration, we will not look at this option in any detail other than to point out that it is a valid option when deadlock has been reached.

What are the traits of a good negotiator?

As well as recognising the best approach, interests or positions to take and when during a negotiation, there are also several other key traits that set aside a good negotiator from the rest of the pack.

Confidence

The appearance of being confident often comes from being well informed on several levels:

- **Objectives** – They not only know what they want to get out of the negotiation, they also have a good idea of what the other side wants to get out of it.
- **People** – They either know who they are going to be negotiating with or they are very quickly able to evaluate them. They also create teams who work well together.
- **Knowledge** – They understand their business and they understand the business of the other parties.
- **Deal Zone** – Before they go into the negotiation, they have a good idea of where a deal can be achieved and, once in the negotiation, they appear to be able to adapt quickly and easily.

In short, they are well prepared.

Credibility

They make deals, even where deals seem impossible, through:

- **Clarity** – There is little confusion about what they are saying or how they say it.
- **Power** – They know how to play the power game to their advantage and how to deflect it when others try it.
- **Empathy** – They will often mirror the language of the other parties, sometimes giving the impression that a particular option they tabled was not theirs but rather that it came from the other party.
- **Controlled** – They are not easily rattled and, in everything they do, they give the impression that they are in complete control.
- **Influencing** – They understand the buttons they need to push and how to push them to get the response they desire.

In short, people believe both in them and in what they are saying.

In Control

Rather than waiting for something to happen, they often appear to be one step ahead, provoking the next step through:

- **Listening** – They understand the needs and wants of the other side, and how these relate to their own needs and wants.
- **Flexibility** – They respond, react and adapt as the negotiation develops, creating options for mutual gain.
- **Momentum** – They build and maintain momentum in a negotiation, heading off any issues before they become sticking points.
- **Managing** – They know the process and the steps required to reach their goal.

In short, they are managing the process rather than letting the process manage them.

What about Power in a Negotiation?

"Power is absolute", *"Power corrupts"* and *"Power is everything"* are all expressions that you may have heard used when people talk about power; but in a negotiation, Power is a very useful tool.

Power comes in many shapes and sizes, and in any negotiation both sides will have some form of power even though they may feel powerless. It is often just a case of recognising it and knowing how to use it.

Sources of Power

There are many sources of power in a negotiation. They may be different from one negotiation to the next, so before each negotiation, you need to take time to work out where your power is going to come from and then how you are going to use it. Some of the sources of power and their uses are:

- **Competition** – some people have a desire to win at all costs which can be a good trait in that is can push them to be the best they can be, but it can also be a negative and may result in them making reactive, potentially desperate decisions just to get the deal. If used in the right context, this source of power can make the counterparty re-evaluate their offer, sometimes before they have even told you what they are looking for, with little effort on your behalf. For example, saying something as simple as "We are looking at two or three other suppliers for this job" could create enough doubt in the supplier's mind to cause a reduction in price before discussions have even started.

- **Edge** – this is also known as your unique selling point, or USP. It is your differentiator or the thing you have or do differently that your competitors don't. It can set you apart and make it difficult to be compared to the market. If your edge is also a key requirement for your counterparty, it can make it very difficult for them to say no, even if your price is higher. For example, a statement such as "What you are looking for is very specialised and there are very few people in the country who can provide it. Fortunately, we are one and we are local" can be enough to get you into pole position.

- **Self-Reliance** – the ability to do something ourselves can help with price or extras, especially in a competitive market. For example, "While we can do this ourselves, we did think it might be useful to see if there is something you can add" is inviting the counterparty to give you something extra to secure the deal.

- **Size** – this can work both ways in that being the biggest has its advantages, such as scale, experience or security, as does being the smallest, such as speed, flexibility and experience. If you are going to use size as a negotiating tool, then you need to closely consider the need or interest. A statement such as "We have a presence in 52 countries around the world" may work well for a multinational but not so well for a small regional organisation.

- **Authority** – Sometimes it can be beneficial not to have the ultimate authority in the room, especially if there are other pressures at play, such as time. Saying "What you are asking for, I do not have the authority to give – but I can agree to..." can lead to the counterparty accepting a deal which is more in your favour.

- **Time** – We have probably all been in a situation where we are running out of time and so we make rash decisions. This has happened to me with birthdays and wedding anniversaries and the gift I ended up selecting was potentially not the best it could have been. Time pressure can have a similar impact during a negotiation. For example, "The gas used within your equipment becomes illegal in four weeks' time, and it will take three and a half weeks to install the replacement. So... the sooner we can reach agreement, the quicker we can help you out" can force the buyer into accepting your proposal.

- **Expertise** – We are often prepared to pay more for expertise; therefore, being able to explain or demonstrate an expertise can help to support a higher fee. For example, "Sue is the only person in the UK who has run this type of project before, and if we can reach an agreement quickly, she will be available to lead the team" may be enough to convince your counterparty to accept a higher fee especially as it is combined with Time.

- **Knowledge** – If it is a choice between you and someone else then finding a source of knowledge that will strengthen your position can help. A contractor I worked with said, "You may be surprised to learn that ten years ago, long before you moved in, we put all the original wiring into this building." The result, their client not only hired them, they also paid extra to get that knowledge.

- **Relationships** – In a similar way to Knowledge, knowing someone, especially someone who is in a higher position within the organisation, can help you secure a better deal. I had one client who would always get to know the most senior people in their target organisations and then drop their names into a sales conversation saying "How's Mary? When you see her can you tell her I said hello and look forward to hearing how her son, Paul, got on at the weekend." While it may seem obvious and something that could be easily defended, it regularly worked as the more junior people didn't want to be the one to turn down the friend of the boss.

- **Position** – This is a great source of power for a buyer, especially in a competitive market. For example, "We have evaluated all the options available and, if you want to continue in this process, you need to alter your position significantly" can result in a supplier dropping their price to win the job or a bidder raising their price.

- **Patience** – if you get the feeling that your counterparty is desperate for work, then saying something like "We don't want to rush into anything" can result in their desperation getting the better of them which can lead to a proposal that is more beneficial for you.

I was involved in a negotiation to provide a service where several of these tactics were used by both parties in two slightly different ways.

We were asked to design a programme for senior management that would be delivered over the next six months. We presented our package and price to the decision makers who we knew were speaking to many other consulting organisations. In fact, they were very keen to stress that they were speaking to other organisations when they first approached us. They had essentially used the competition source of power in an attempt to make us question our fees before the pitch.

During our preparation, we took all factors into consideration and decided that we would not discount our fees. We knew this could be a risk, but we were confident in our offering and we also had our own source of power in that we had alternatives if this project did not come through.

A couple of weeks after our presentation we received an email saying Thank you for your very well thought out programme but in this case, you are too expensive. However, if you are still interested in carrying out this project, could you sharpen your pencil?"

The door had not been completely closed on us, so our planning, some might call it a gamble, had paid off and we were still in with a chance.

In their email, once again they were using competition as a source of power to try to get me to reduce our fees. In this case, the phrase "too expensive" was how they tried to influence us. Unfortunately, it was used without any qualification which can be a sign that the person saying it is not very confident in it. So, we were left wondering if we were too expensive when compared to the other offers or just too expensive in general?

One response could have been to simply say no, that is our price, take it or leave it. Essentially, we could have taken a positional approach and tough it out. In this case, we had a long-term relationship with the client, and so I decided to take an interest-based approach and asked if I could come in to talk to them.

In advance of this meeting, I used all the planning tools we will look at in a later section of this book, including getting buy-in from senior management to the idea of walking away if I had to go below our red line. As a result, I went in fully confident of winning the business, remaining very profitable and maintaining the good working relationship.

Once the social niceties had been completed at the start of the meeting, they once again used the unqualified "too expensive" line and said that they were looking forward to hearing my revised offer. Rather than answering that question, I took control of the meeting by telling them that before I get to that, I just had a couple of questions.

Firstly, was there anything they wanted to change about the content of the programme. If the answer was yes, then changing the package could present the perfect opportunity to offer a revised price. The answer I received was "No, everything is great, in fact management much prefers your proposal." The balance of power had just shifted slightly towards me as I felt that senior management had already made the emotional decision to use us.

Next, I wanted to check the qualification criteria for "too expensive", so I asked if the content of any of the other offers were the same as ours? Again, if the answer was yes, then I would go on to try to find out if our price was the highest of all the offers. In this case, they came back with "No, your programme was the most comprehensive". So, I now knew that management wanted us, and we had an edge over the competition. It was becoming clear that this was more a situation of "Just get something off the price".

I asked one final multi-part question that was designed to build some pressure, and then provide an easy release. I said, "You told me that we were too expensive. Can you tell me the prices quoted by the other organisations?" I then paused for a second, just enough time to see an expression that said, I don't know how to answer, and I continued "Sorry, I don't expect you to answer that, but, are we a million miles off?" The look of relief that came across their face as the said "no, you are not" told me all I needed to know. I then told them the discount I was prepared to provide, they said thank you very much and on that basis, we are happy to proceed, and our profit margin only dropped by 2%.

How Do I Deal with 'Non-Negotiables'?

If your counterparty claims that something is non-negotiable then you have four options:

1. Try using a concession. We will look at concessions in much more detail later, but for now, consider a concession as something you are prepared to trade to get what you want. Some of the concessions that may be available are:

   - Price
   - Terms
   - Quantity
   - Added extras
   - Schedule
   - Guarantees
   - Location
   - Service
   - Features
   - Long-term support
   - Insurance
   - Small print
   - Follow-up work

2. Accept the deal as it is. The offer that is being made may be the best you will get and if you have been unable to get the other party to move, then accept it. Be careful that you don't

let your ego take over. Because we feel that we didn't get everything we wanted, we make a foolish, emotional decision and walk away when the logical choice is to accept the offer.

3. Use one of the keys to unlock deadlock. If the counterparty is saying that something is not negotiable, this is a deadlock. We will look at this in more detail, but some of the keys include:
   - Change the people
   - Change the location
   - Get higher authority involved
   - Take a break to reflect

4. Walk away. If the deal is not better than your red line or you have a better offer, then tell the counterparty that you are going to walk away. This can force them to open-up negotiations, or it can result in them walking away as well. You need to make sure that you are prepared to walk away as this is a very difficult situation to recover.

Key Takeaways

A negotiation:

- is a discussion that is intended to reach an agreement.
- needs to have two or more parties, something to talk about and your own red line clearly identified.
- can be based on positions or interests or a combination of both.
- will run better for you if you are well prepared, viewed as credible in the eyes of the counterparty, and are able to manage the process.
- can be tilted in your favour by using power but you should also be aware that the counterparty may try to use power as well.
- may have items that are non-negotiable. Test that assertion / assumption and if it is better than your red line, you may have to accept it.

Further Thought

Some negotiations are reasonably straightforward, some are complex, and others are feel like they will never end. Reflect on your past negotiations; see if you can identify the approach that was taken and if there was anything you would do differently if you could do it again.

About You, The Negotiator

In the previous section, we had a look at what might be described as some of the hard, technical elements of a negotiation. In this section, we are going to look at the soft, people elements – because we should separate the people from the deal. Despite it often turning out this way, negotiations should not become personal.

As soon as possible, establish a process and agree on the way you are going to approach the negotiation. If everyone on all sides is happy with the approach, you have a better chance of reaching an agreement. In other words, face the problem and not the people.

To do this, consider the following three areas:

- Perception
    - Put yourself in their position
    - Don't blame them for your problem
    - Share your views with them
    - Take advantage of opportunities to show them that something they perceive to be an area of conflict cannot be based on new data provided by you
    - Make sure your solutions are consistent with their values

- Emotion
  - Understand their emotion and be in control of your own
  - Don't draw conclusions about their intentions based on your own emotional state – such as fear or relief.
  - Don't react to their emotional outbursts
  - Let them cool off, or back off emotionally

- Communication
  - Build a dialogue
  - Use active listening techniques to engage fully with the other side
  - Speak with the intention to be understood
  - Focus what you say on yourself and your issues, not on them. This way you can inform them of your needs.

The Negotiator's Tasks

If you are negotiating alone then there are three main tasks you must perform during the discussion that is intended to reach an agreement:

- Communicate
- Take Notes
- Manage the Negotiation

These might seem obvious, but if they are not done correctly, there is a real risk that the result from the negotiation will not be as desired.

Communicate

I have yet to meet anybody who likes to be talked **at**; we all like to be talked **with** in a respectful way. So, try to take advantage of the balance provided by nature: two ears and one mouth. But I am also going to throw into the mix two eyes and one, comparatively, very large body. It is important to not underestimate the messages sent via body language.

Communication is a two-way process, involving a transmitter and a receiver (the talker and the listener), and for each of these parties, communication is done on two levels – verbally and physically. Recognising these levels is enormously important in a negotiation.

Transmit

When we are talking in a negotiation, or for that matter in a meeting, we need to be very careful about the messages we are sending. Those messages are sent on two levels, verbally and non-verbally. We will look at body language in more detail in a later section, but for the moment I want to look at the interaction between what you say and how you say it.

First, you need to make sure that you don't send mixed messages – for example, smiling while delivering bad news or looking at your shoes while trying to look like you mean something.

Next, choose your words wisely. Make sure that whatever you say can be, and is, understood by the other side. If you want to make a firm point, don't use soft language.

Finally, don't spend all your time on transmit: build a dialogue that allows the counterparty to appear to take the lead.

Receive

When you are listening to the other party, not only do you need to listen to what they are saying, you also need to be aware of how they are saying it. In other words, you need to be listening **and** watching.

First, listen to what they are saying and make sure that you understand it and that it is consistent. Don't be frightened to ask for clarification.

Next, when they are talking, don't interrupt; let them talk until they are finished and then wait a little bit and watch them. You may pick up some signs, and that little bit of silence might make them start talking again.

Finally, look to see if their body is supporting what they are saying. When they are sounding confident, are they looking confident? There are a few phrases that signal an incongruency. But be careful – it may just be a phrase that the person uses as part of their everyday language.

These phrases are:

- *To be honest* – Everything I have said before may have been a bit less than truthful, and I am now going to appeal to your sense of fairness.
- *I am sure you already know this* – What follows might be something that I am going to try to slip in. I am trying to make it seem insignificant when in actual fact it may not be.
- *Would it surprise you...?* – What I am about to say now is intended to be a surprise, and I am looking to use it to apply some pressure.

- *But...* – What I am going to say now is going to take away all the good things that I have just said. Perhaps I am going to apply the Influencing Principle of Scarcity, which is described later.

Take Notes

Unless you are in a team situation, you cannot rely on someone else to record what is going on during the discussion.

You need to record not just what is being said, but also how it is being said – the non-verbal indications.

You need to note down everything that happens during the negotiation, such as any agreements and concessions (including the order in which they are being given/requested), plus positions and adjournments.

One layout that works very well is the multi-column layout. Here you have a column for each party and you make notes, sequentially, in the column for the party who is transmitting. Any agreements can be noted on the line in the middle, and by following the flow of the notes, you will be able to see how that agreement came about.

Multi-Column Notes Layout

A word of caution about taking notes with an example from the legal world and another from private equity. I was observing a lawyer who was taking notes during a negotiation and from the amount of writing, it was clear that they were going to be very detailed. Unfortunately, it also became very clear when something important was said because the lawyer drew a box around it in their notes. It didn't take long to work out what was important to them and how we could use it to our advantage. In the private equity example, there were no notes being taken, unless something was being said that they wanted. We knew they wanted it because you could clearly see items on a list being ticked off. These cautionary tales should not deter you from taking notes, but rather serve as a warning to find a method that works well without damaging the negotiation.

Manage the Negotiation

In most circumstances in a negotiation, you need to build and maintain momentum without losing control of the process. This is a careful balancing act and can require you to give the other party freedom go where they want to without allowing them to take control of the negotiation. The Negotiation Framework, detailed later in this book, will help you achieve this.

You need to maintain a balance between the parties and keep an eye on time. It is very easy, when the pressure is on, to lose track of where you are in terms of time, and as a result, you can end up putting unnecessary pressure on yourself.

All adjournments need to be properly managed. They are not intended to be review sessions; they are planning sessions, and you need to make sure of that.

Earlier we said that one of the traits of an expert negotiator was that they always appeared to be in control. This is true whether they are in the planning, negotiating or reviewing phase. They know where they are going and how they are going to get there. We will look at the process in more detail later, but for now, here is a high-level framework for control.

A High-Level Framework for Control

To be in control of a negotiation, you need to understand the fundamental framework within which any negotiation will operate. At a high level, this framework consists of three basic blocks:

- *Pre-Negotiation Planning* – prepare everything we need to go into the negotiation, such as objectives, initial positions, information we are prepared to share, questions we want to ask, concessions we want, concessions we are prepared to trade, who will be in the parties, where it will be held, what the layout of the room will be and so on

- *Negotiating* – our discussion that is intended to reach an agreement.

- *Post-Negotiation Reviewing* – don't make the mistake of assuming that once the negotiation has concluded, either successfully or unsuccessfully, that you are finished. Great negotiators recognise and understand the value of reviewing all negotiations, and will perform this review using three main categories that are expanded upon later:
  - o People
  - o Process
  - o Positions

The Negotiator's Behaviour

The way you behave in a negotiation will go a long way towards establishing the atmosphere in the negotiation and the responses from the other parties.

Regardless of which approach, interests, or positions you decide to take in the negotiation, you should follow these simple guidelines:

Ask Questions

The more information you can obtain from the other party, the better equipped you will be to make decisions. You need to ask open questions to try to get a G.R.I.P of the conversation and encourage dialogue:

- **G**et going – ask questions that will start a conversation
- **R**evealing – based on what you find out from the opening questions, ask some that start to reveal what the counterparty is looking for
- **I**nterests based – now try to understand the interests that are the drivers behind what they have revealed
- **P**ositional – finally ask questions that will help to reveal the positions that might be acceptable

A **G**et going question could be as simple as "What are you looking for?" This starts the conversation. I have sat in many negotiations where the counterparty has just started to talk at me or about themselves without any indication that they are interested in me. This could possibly taint the negotiation from the start.

Once you have found out what the other party is looking for, start to ask questions that will help Reveal more information. For example, if they were to tell me that they are looking to improve their sales people, then I might ask, "Tell me more about your current sales process?" This could result in them telling me all about their process without saying what is wrong with it, so I will ask some Interests based questions to understand why they feel it could be better.

Finally, once I have listened carefully to their answer I would ask a Positional question such as "So, if we were able to observe the process in action and create some specific adjustments, either to the general process or to how the individual salespeople operate, would that be beneficial?" This final question is designed to suggest a solution without committing to it and the answer will help to identify the counterparty's desire. For example, if their answer was "Absolutely!" then you know what they really want, but if their answer was "Well, in a way yes" then you would take a step back and ask another Revealing or Interests based question.

Listen

This might seem like an obvious thing to say, but listen to hear what the other party is actually saying, not what you think they are saying. Many misunderstandings come from the fact that one side has not really heard what the other side has said. Instead, they hear what they *expect* to hear or *want* to hear.

For example, let's say you have been asked to meet with a potential client to discuss a piece of work, and they tell you how happy they are that you came in to see them. They are really interested to hear more about how you could help them. What you may hear is that you are the only person they are talking to about this opportunity but all they have said is tell us about how you can help them.

Whether you have asked a question or you are just having a conversation, listen carefully to ensure that you are actually hearing and understanding what they are really saying. Once you have heard what the counterparty has said, evaluate it against what you have just said, were expecting or have already heard throughout the negotiation, and work out what you are going to do next.

If you need to ask for clarity, do it. There is no point in thinking after the meeting, "I wish I had asked..."

Don't "Hog the Floor"

If we follow the first two behaviours, this one won't really be a problem. Resist the temptation to monologue. A negotiation is all about building dialogue.

I used to work with a person who liked to talk a lot, especially about themselves. The two of us went to see a potential client and despite all our planning, he decided that day would be his off day. After our meeting, this colleague expressed that he felt the meeting had gone very well. A couple of days later, I received a phone call telling me that they really didn't understand what we had to offer as Mr X spent the meeting talking over me and so they decided to go with someone else.

At the same time, don't allow yourself to be dominated by your counterparty. Make sure you keep a balance and, if necessary, be strong enough to re-establish control by guiding them back to the topic at hand or closing that discussion and moving onto the next item.

Summarise Regularly

When things are moving quickly in a negotiation, it becomes very easy to lose sight of the current positions. Summarising and checking for agreement on the situation are very effective ways of making sure that all parties are at the same place. It also prevents one side from coming back at the end and claiming that they didn't agree to something.

Also, when progress appears to have stalled, summarising can be a very effective way of getting the negotiation moving again.

Build the Relationship

This is really all about building on common ground rather than pointing out differences. You don't have to build a relationship to the point where you would be happy for your respective families to take a holiday together. All you need to do is to build a working relationship based on mutual respect.

Control Your Emotions

Be careful that you remain in control of your emotions. Do not allow your emotions to control you. Make sure that you do not lose control by responding to threats and abuse with threats and abuse, no matter how mad or frustrated you feel. That is not the time to unleash your inner beast. Sure, you should tell them to stop or even display anger, but you need to remain in control.

Another area of emotion I frequently get asked about is the "poker face", the completely unemotional, flat and unresponsive face. I often get told by clients that their "poker face" is not great and that they would like to improve it. I take these clients through a little exercise where I get them to try to convince me of something or sell me something simple, like a pad of paper or a pen, and I just sit there staring blankly, not responding in any way. After a couple of minutes, I ask them how that felt, and the answers range from frustrating to intimidating to wanting to shake some life into me! Showing no emotion is not an asset and can actually damage the relationship of all those involved in the negotiation. There can be a time, however, to not show emotion; for example, if you are presented with the best offer ever and you smile and then tell them it is not good enough. In this case, an emotionless response followed by a simple statement such as "That is not good enough" can be enough to put pressure back onto them and force them into making a concession.

In general, I believe that allowing the other side to know how hard you are working for them, how difficult you are finding something or how excited you are about a move they have made can help to keep the negotiation going and build a collaborative environment.

Look for Options for Mutual Gain

Work with the other party to build on common ground and keep the negotiation moving forward. Ensure that whatever you do is mutually beneficial. Avoid building your position too aggressively or giving ground away to the other party.

To find options for mutual, gain try:

- Treating their problems as if they are your own, helping them to find solutions – if you were in their shoes, what would you do? The answer to this might be to walk away from the piece of work, and while you may miss out financially, the relationship and their trust in you will have greatly increased. This could be important for future transactions.

- Work on options to broaden the topic in line with each party's interest. This is similar to brainstorming, described below, with the exception that it is about understanding objectives and expectations and then working out where the overlaps exist and how to bridge any gaps.

- Make their choices clear and easy to understand – use straightforward language in the first place or provide all the information they need. Ask them to describe the solution in their own words. If they can articulate your proposal in their own words, they are more likely to have made the connection to their benefits.

- Brainstorm to find more answers before making decisions – asking questions such as "if you could start again, what would you do differently" or "what have you tried before" or "what are other people doing" can help people think outside of the box.

- Understanding their preferences – ask questions that are focused on *their* interests or reasons rather than on the potential solution.

Personal Style

While we are all individuals and react differently depending on the position we find ourselves in, Merrill and Reid[2] identified four basic social styles that carry across to negotiations. These styles are based on two dimensions:

- *Assertiveness* – The degree to which a person attempts to control situations or the thoughts and actions of others.

- *Responsiveness* – The readiness with which a person outwardly displays emotions or feelings and develops relationships.

These combine to give a two-dimensional model of behaviour which will help you not only understand how others perceive you but also work out how you can deal more effectively with different styles.

---

[2] *"Knowing About Social Styles" developed by Merrill and Reid*

The Assertiveness Scale

This measures the degree to which a person is seen as attempting to influence the thoughts, decisions or actions of others, either directly by talking or indirectly by questioning.

- "Tell" behaviour is risk-taking, fast-paced, challenging.
- "Ask" behaviour is cooperative, deliberate and minimises risks.

Assertive people are confident and know what they want. They are not afraid to put forward their opinion or of conflict. They will be more than happy to argue their case.

In the extreme, this can cause problems in a negotiation because highly assertive people can appear to be aggressive which can result in friction between the parties and, ultimately, a breakdown in the relationship.

On the flipside, people who lack or have low assertiveness can be viewed as a bit of a pushover and, as a result, get taken advantage of by the more assertive people around the table.

The Responsiveness Scale

This measures the degree to which a person either openly expresses their feelings or controls their feelings. The ends of the scale are "control" and "emote".

- "Control" behaviour is disciplined, serious and cool.
- "Emote" behaviour is relationship-oriented, open and warm.

Responsive people are likely to be open communicators, responding to both questions and people.

This can have a downside for negotiation as highly responsive people are more likely to give more information away than they intended to and as a result may harm their positions.

At the other end of the scale, people can appear to be negative or difficult, often unwilling or unable to respond to attempts to build a relationship.

People who score very highly on the assertiveness scale can be intimidating to those who score highly on the responsiveness scale. In a negotiation, this can lead to the responsive people agreeing just to get out of the situation.

I recently worked with a Responsive client who found himself doing anything to get out of meetings where a certain Assertive person was present. Actually, he would do anything he could to avoid the meetings in the first place. The Assertive person thought the meetings were great and couldn't understand why the Responsive person was so quiet and uninterested in the meeting. Understanding the different styles became a breakthrough moment for both of them. They suddenly understood each other's preferences and how to work more effectively together. And the meetings became massively more productive with both people actively engaged.

Along with understanding the Responsive and Assertiveness scale, the rest of this section will look at Four Negotiation Styles, their preferences and how they can more effectively interact with each other.

The Four Negotiation Styles

The negotiation styles I have identified are adapted from the four styles originally defined by Merrill and Reid. They can be graphically represented as shown below.

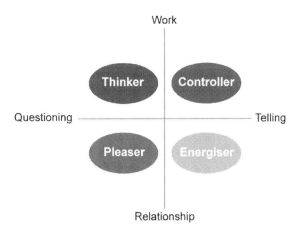

Negotiating Styles

The Thinker and Controller are more focussed on the job at hand whereas the Pleaser and Energiser are more interested in their relationships.

The Controller and Energiser are more assertive than the Thinker and Pleaser.

The Controller is more likely to tell you what they want whereas the Thinker is more likely to ask for the steps to get the job done.

The Pleaser is more likely to ask how the product will help or benefit other people whereas the Energiser is more likely to tell you how they want it to benefit them.

In the context of a negotiation this means that:

- **The Thinker** needs to have all the information before making a decision and will take time to make that decision.
- **The Pleaser** likes to know that the decision they are making is safe and wants to understand how it will impact on others.
- **The Controller** wants to be in charge and have all decisions be based on their objectives.
- **The Energiser** wants to know how the decision will impact on them without getting bogged down in detail.

The rest of the section outlines each of the styles including how best to negotiate with them.

The Thinker

Thinker people can appear unsociable, especially to the Pleaser and the Energiser.

They may seem serious and indecisive because they need to look at every conceivable angle before they feel satisfied. A consequence of this is that they are persistent in their questioning and focus on detail and facts.

However, once they have decided, they stick with their decision as they invariably feel that it is infallible.

They have a basic need to be correct and when in conflict, they can whine, become sarcastic and are often negative. When you recognise this behaviour, keep to the facts, don't just agree with them and listen attentively.

They measure success and personal value through accuracy and especially in being right.

They take time to be accurate and will present benefits around how they will work.

They make decisions based on evidence and experience that support their principles and thinking.

The Thinker's Characteristics
On an emotional, personal level they can appear to be:

- Deep and thoughtful
- Serious and purposeful
- Idealistic
- Appreciate of beauty
- Sensitivity to others
- Self-sacrificing
- Conscientious
- Remembering the negatives
- Too introspective
- Depressed, even moody
- Insecure
- Rigid
- Stuffy

In a work situation they can:

- Appear schedule or detail-oriented
- Be orderly and well organised
- Appear frustrated if things are not done right
- Prefer charts, figures, etc.
- Set high standards
- Be persistent and thorough
- Finish what they start, sometimes before starting something else

- Be more task than people oriented
- Be hard to please, rigid
- Spend too much time planning
- Prefer analysis to action
- Become depressed at or frustrated by imperfection
- Be self-deprecating
- Have a deep need for approval

Negotiation Tips for the Thinker

If you are a Thinker, you may want to consider the following when dealing with other people who have a different style:

- The Controller – keep things moving. The Controller likes to keep a fast pace with a focus on an outcome. As a Thinker, you will want to take your time and explore all possibilities. However, you should pick one that will work and focus on aligning that with the Controller's aims.
- The Pleaser – align with their priorities. The Pleaser needs to feel that the decision aligns with their beliefs and experiences so talk in terms of security even though you may tend to think more in terms of the facts.
- The Energiser – keep things moving and align with their priorities. The Energiser needs to

have a high tempo and doesn't want to get bogged down in details. They also tend to make decisions based on what they believe is right and very often it is more about them than the wider team.

When dealing with another Thinker, you may want to consider the following:

- Make sure it does not turn into paralysis by analysis. There is a risk that the level of analysis required to make a decision will be high. Try to identify the best routes to take and focus on that, avoiding unnecessary investigations.

When Negotiating with the Thinker

To give the Thinker the best opportunity to get to the outcome you are looking for, try to:

- Focus on past, present and future
- Talk facts
- Focus on detail and accuracy
- Be logical and well-organised
- Tell them exactly what you will do and when
- Allow time to ponder
- Give them all the evidence, facts, figures, examples that they need to be assured of being right

The Pleaser

The Pleaser likes other people's company, though is more of a listener than a talker.

They are loyal, personable and show patience when dealing with other people.

They may not be perceived as people *who get things done* because they can spend more time developing relationships rather than getting down to business.

They are also unlikely to take risks as they need to have a feeling of security that they are doing the right thing.

When things get difficult, a Pleaser is more likely to want to avoid the situation and can lack conviction which may mean that if pushed, they are likely to make promises they cannot keep.

The Controller often finds them frustrating because they want a straight answer and the Pleaser can find this difficult to deliver.

They have a basic need for security so reassure and support them and take every opportunity to confirm your commitment to them and the deal.

They measure success and personal values through a feeling of security in that they have made the right decision.

They take time to be agreeable and will present benefits around why the outcome will be good.

They make decisions based on guarantees and assurances that support their relationships and feelings.

Their Characteristics

On an emotional, personal level, they can appear to be:

- Low-key, quiet, but witty
- Calm, cool and collected
- Sympathetic and kind
- Patient and well-balanced
- Easy-going and relaxed
- Happily reconciled to life
- Emotionally guarded
- Unenthusiastic, shy
- Indecisive
- Too compromising
- Self-righteous
- Fearful, worried and want to avoid responsibility

In a work situation, they can:

- Be competent and steady

- Display administrative ability
- Avoid conflict
- Find the easy way
- Be peaceful and agreeable
- Mediate problems
- Be good under pressure
- Not be goal-oriented
- Lack self-motivation
- Be lazy and careless
- Prefer to be a spectator
- Be hard to get moving
- Resent being pushed
- Discourage others

Negotiation Tips for the Pleaser

If you are a Pleaser, you may want to consider the following when dealing with other people who have a different style:

- The Thinker – align with their priorities. As a Pleaser, you need to feel that the decision aligns with your beliefs whereas the Thinker needs to understand the rational facts that support the decision.
- The Controller – keep if fast paced and align with their priorities. The Controller likes to make decisions based on objectives. Whatever

you are trying to get them to agree to, make sure it aligns with their objectives.

- The Energiser – keep it fast paced. The Energiser wants to build and maintain a fast pace so make sure the discussion does not slow down. It would be better to take a break than spend a long time deliberating in the room.

When dealing with another Pleaser, you may want to consider the following:

- Make a decision. Pleasers often want to feel that they have made the correct decision and so will defer making that decision until they have sought reassurance. If necessary, get others involved early.

When Negotiating with the Pleaser
To give the Pleaser the best opportunity to get to the outcome you are looking for, try to:

- Focus on tradition
- Be flexible with your approach
- Be easy and informal
- Be personal and personable
- Give them time to feel good about your offer
- Emphasise that it is a team approach
- Stress how they can feel safe in making the decision

The Controller

The Controller is task orientated and expect efficiency from everyone they encounter.

Little emphasis is placed on building relationships with other people.

They can be perceived as aggressive and uncaring, especially by the Pleaser, but this can be useful as they are prepared to take risks and push things through.

They have a basic need to be in control and so when in conflict, they will try to steam roll over anyone who comes in their way, so it is important to be assertive and firm and have a solution to the problem but also listen to them.

They measure success and personal values by results and want a climate that allows them to build their own environment, plan and structures.

The Controller takes time to be efficient and will present benefits around what they will achieve.

They make decisions based on options and probabilities that support their actions and conclusions.

Their Characteristics

On an emotional, personal level they can appear to be:

- Unemotional, independent and self-sufficient
- Strong-willed and decisive
- A change junkie
- Keen to correct wrongs
- Very confident
- Not easily discouraged
- Bossy, insensitive
- Quick-tempered
- Impatient and can't relax
- Enjoying an argument
- Unable to give up when losing
- Unsympathetic
- Unhappy at a show of emotions

In a work situation, they can:

- Be goal-oriented
- See the whole picture
- Be organised and plan ahead
- Motivate people to action
- Seek practical solutions
- Insist on outputs and results
- Thrive on opposition
- Believe that the end justifies the means

- Over dominate
- Not analyse the details
- Make rush decisions
- Manipulate other people
- Be intolerant of mistakes
- Be a workaholic

Negotiation Tips for the Controller

If you are a Controller, you may want to consider the following when dealing with other people who have a different style:

- The Thinker – give them time. The Thinker likes to have time to make decisions and to ensure that they have weighed up all the possibilities. As a Controller, there can be a desire to get things done quickly and your way.
- The Pleaser – give them time and align with their priorities. As with the Thinker, the Pleaser does not like to be rushed; they need to have time to make decisions. They also need to feel that the decision aligns with their beliefs.
- The Energiser – align with their priorities. The Energiser tends to make decisions based on what they believe is right and very often it is more about them than the wider team.

When dealing with another Controller, you may want to consider the following:

- Make sure it does not become a competition. The other person may want to take the conversation in a completely different direction. You need to take time and consider the situation before deciding to let them feel they are in control or take control back by, amongst others, taking a break, steering the conversation back to the agenda or asking questions related to your objectives.

When Negotiating with the Controller

To give the Controller the best opportunity to get to the outcome you are looking for, try to:

- Focus on the present
- Be brief and efficient
- Get to the bottom line quickly
- Speak in terms of short-term, concrete results
- Give them options that work towards results
- Let them feel in control by giving them time to speak and work with timescales
- Stress how they will win

The Energiser

The Energiser likes the company of other people, though unlike the Pleaser, this is because they need to '*express*' themselves.

The Pleaser can support and enhance them very well, but if the Energiser becomes too aggressive or forceful, it can make the Pleaser back off and become a silent and potentially unsupportive partner.

They can be good people to have involved in a negotiation because they're enthusiastic and can often become creative and find innovative ways to move forward.

They have a basic need for recognition. As a result, when they are in conflict situations, they can become emotional, prone to exaggeration and in the worst case, unpredictable. This can make them very difficult to deal with and can derail negotiations. The best way to deal with this is to give them time to calm down and don't say anything to reignite the negative feelings.

They measure success and personal values by immediate feedback.

They like to be stimulating and will frame any benefits around the ones that will be impacted by them.

The Energiser makes intuitive decisions based on success stories and incentives which support their aspirations.

Their Characteristics

On an emotional, personal level they can appear to be:

- Emotional and demonstrative
- Living in the present
- Talkative and a good storyteller
- Curious
- Humorous and have a sincere heart
- Capture and engage with listeners
- Egotistical and exaggerative
- Childish, naive and gullible
- Fake and flimsy
- Weak-willed, reactive and restless

In a work situation, they can:

- Be the first to volunteer to do things
- Like to start meetings or presentations in a flashy way
- Have and create energy and enthusiasm
- Think on their feet and create new activities
- Be creative and colourful

- Look great on the outside
- Charm others into doing things
- Prefer to talk rather than do and so waste time
- Be disorganised and undisciplined
- Make decisions based on feelings
- Get priorities out of order, putting personal aspirations before business
- Forget the promises they made.
- Become easily distracted.
- Find their confidence drops quickly when under pressure or when confronted.

Negotiating Tips for the Energiser

If you are an Energiser, you may want to consider the following when dealing with other people who have a different style:

- The Thinker – give them time. The Thinker likes to have time to make decisions and to ensure that they have weighed up all the possibilities. As an Energiser, you can have a desire to get things done quickly and without thought for the details.
- The Pleaser – give them time and align with their priorities. As with the Thinker, the Pleaser does not like to be rushed, they need to

have time to make decisions. They also need to feel that the decision aligns with their beliefs

- The Controller – align with their priorities. The Controller tends to make decisions based on how the outcome aligns with an objective rather than with a feeling.

When dealing with another Energiser, you may want to consider the following:

- Keep it focused. With another Energiser, there is a real risk that the conversation will go off topic and that decisions will be made without really thinking it through. Focus on the desired outcome and if necessary, get others involved.

When Negotiating with the Energiser

To give the Energiser the best opportunity to get to the outcome you are looking for, try to:

- Focus on the future
- Illustrate concepts with stories they can relate to
- Seek their ideas and input into the creation of the final package

- Focus on the big picture and find out who will help fill in the details
- Show interest in the things that are of interest to them
- Stimulate their creative impulse by asking them questions that access their imagination
- Compliment them and their ideas
- Stress how they will stand out from others, especially the people they measure themselves against

What is My Negotiation Style?

First of all, there is nothing better or worse about any of the four styles so don't feel that you have to fit into the Thinker or Controller style to be a good negotiator. Each style has its positive attributes that need to be continually reinforced and built upon, and each has its negative ones that need to be kept under control.

To understand your negotiation style, look back through the style descriptions and check off the attributes that you feel reflect you in a negotiation. Count the number of ticks for each style and this will give you an indication of the balance of your Negotiation Style.

Team Negotiations

Sometimes having someone with us in the negotiation can be beneficial. There are many reasons for adopting a team approach and if any of the following are relevant, then you should probably consider setting up a negotiation team rather than going solo.

Reasons for having a team:

- It provides an extra set of eyes to observe behaviours and identify non-verbal communications.
- You need help in planning. This may not be because of a lack of knowledge; it may be due to time constraints, or it may be useful to have another opinion to challenge your natural biases.
- The Negotiator's tasks of managing the process and taking notes can be distributed to someone else, leaving you free to concentrate on the task of negotiating.
- There is simply strength in numbers and having someone else with you can help to build your confidence.
- It gives the opportunity for in-negotiation brainstorming. While there are advantages to taking adjournments to plan, if you want to keep things moving, then having someone to talk to in the negotiation or someone who may

be able to come up with creative solutions can help.

- For some areas of the package, it may be necessary to have specific expertise. For example, if I have no expertise in International Tax but one element of the negotiation requires this skillset, then I will bring in an expert. Another reason may be to bring in someone who has more of a reputation or a well-known name as this can add weight to an argument.
- If there is an existing relationship with one of your colleagues, then it may be good to involve them so that there is familiarity or continuity.
- Create a better combination of negotiating styles. If your primary style is one that is task focussed, then to provide balance, you may want to take someone with you who is more relationship focused, especially if that is the style of your counterparty.

If you have decided to create a team, then it is important to recognise that there are four areas that require clarity and alignment:

- Goals and Objectives – make sure that all team members are pulling in the same direction and fully support the same set of goals and objectives. If team members are pulling in different directions and are only interested in satisfying their own needs, then there is a real risk that the team will fail.

- Roles and Responsibilities – clearly identify what each person is going to be doing. This will stop people talking across and potentially contradicting each other.

- Procedures and Strategies – what are the procedures you are going to follow? For example, all decisions must be approved by a committee before final sign-off or the team will break to assess the offer once we have identified their key wants. You should also set out the strategy you are going to adopt and the role each will play. For example, if you are going to use the Good Cop / Bad Cop power play then identify who will play which role in advance and stick to it at the start.

- Relationships and Styles – is the relationship between each of the team members good? Cracks can appear under the pressure of a negotiations so take time to build the relationships in your own team. Do you have a good balance of styles? For example, having two Thinkers could slow down the process as both may want to discuss more detail than is necessary to get agreement.

For all of these, clarity and alignment can be achieved through effective planning – but beware, as this will take time and energy to do properly.

Finally, there are also disadvantages to a team approach that you should consider, and these are:

- There is an extra mouth that needs to be controlled. If we are honest, we have all stopped ourselves from saying something that we know we will later regret. Some, like me, may also have worked with people who have said something that the team also regretted. It is important that we not only prepare what we are going to say but what we should avoid saying.

- More planning time will be required as, once diaries can be aligned, there will be more discussion around the topics.

- Unfortunately, people can come in with hidden agendas, some of which can be to deliberately undermine you. This may seem hard to believe, but I have worked with people who are only interested in furthering their own career, sometimes to the detriment of the wider organisation. Be careful of who you want to have on your team.

- Too many options created during planning or the negotiation can result in a lack of focus and confusion as to what has been agreed. Pick the right toys from your toy box.

Deciding Solo or Team

Early in planning, one of the questions you need to answer is: "Will I be negotiating by myself or will I need to bring others with me?" The answer to this question can often be forced upon you when there is no one to help or you are expected to bring a team. Whichever of these two situations applies, look at the topics you will be discussing to help you identify the areas where you might need help. Moreover, when combined with the following situations, it will be beneficial to take a team approach:

- The negotiation is complex, requiring a diverse set of knowledge, abilities, or expertise.
- The negotiation has great potential for creative, integrative solutions.
- Diverse constituencies and interests must be represented at the table, as in union negotiations.
- You want to display your strength to the other side – for example, in international contexts where teams are expected.
- You want to signal to the other side that you take the negotiation very seriously, as in a merger or acquisition.
- You trust and respect available team members.

- You have sufficient time to organise and coordinate a team effort.

Team Roles

Before we look at the roles in detail, it is important to point out that these are roles, not people. If you are a solo negotiator then you will have to fulfil all these roles. If there are two in the team, then you can split the roles.

The first three of the four following roles are key and need to be fulfilled regardless of the number of people in the team.

Administrator

The Administrator role is responsible for managing the process from planning to review. During the negotiation, this role allows the Negotiator role to focus on conducting the negotiation by managing the meeting. The role does not always have to be fulfilled by the most senior person, but this can prove beneficial.

In summary, this role should:

- Manage the planning, negotiation and review
- Listen to what the counterparties are saying

- Watch for signs, such as body language, from the counterparties
- Recognise and manage conflict

Finally, if this role is fulfilled by the most senior person in the negotiation, they could cover introductions and help to move the negotiation from the more social elements to business.

Negotiator

This role is responsible for the negotiation and will lead all communications during the negotiation. This also means that the role must be filled at the very start of planning and this person must attend all planning meetings. The role will be empowered by the team/company to act on their behalf, discovering information, positioning, trading concessions and getting agreement.

In summary, this role should:

- Attend and provide input to all planning and review sessions
- Lead the negotiation
- Draw up and agree the package
- Give and get information
- Deliver and respond to positions
- Trade concessions
- Get agreement

Observer

This role is responsible for watching the counterparties and recording what is being communicated both verbally and physically. It is essentially a silent role that should only speak to gain clarification. The role should provide input into any planning sessions and adjournments and needs to understand the proposed package.

In summary, this role should:

- Observe and record the counterparty's communication
- Note agreements
- Summarise, if requested
- Ask questions to clarify, when necessary
- Provide input into planning, adjournments and review sessions

Expert

This is very much a support role within the team and needs to be there for specific reasons, such as technical or legal expertise. The role needs to contribute, when requested, so needs to attend planning meetings.

In summary, this role should:

- Have a reason to be fulfilled

- Provide input into planning and review sessions
- Provide input when required

I am sure we can all think of times when the team we were part of has not performed particularly well. I am even sure that some of you can think of times that the team performed disastrously, so let me relay a short story about a well prepared and supportive team. A local government department was preparing for a contractor to come in and deliver the costs for a contract extension. They were fully prepared for the contractor to try to up the price, so they all agreed to flinch as soon as they heard the offer and then say nothing. The time came, the contractor delivered their proposal, and as one, the local government team all sighed, shook their heads and looked at the contractor. Almost immediately the contractor said "Hang on... I mean... well... we can drop that to..." and within 30 seconds the team had saved almost £280k just by being well prepared and acting as one.

Key Takeaways

A good negotiator:

- communicates effectively, observing as well as listening and reinforcing what they are saying with non-verbal communication
- will not go into a negotiation blind but will prepare and will review the outcomes to understand what they can learn
- will get a GRIP of the negotiation through effective questioning
- will ensure that the counterparty has plenty of opportunities to get their points across
- will use emotions throughout the negotiation without losing control of them
- will build and reinforce the relationship through options for mutual gain
- can identify different styles and knows their preferences and how to use them to their advantage
- works well in a team situation by having clearly identified roles and responsibilities

Further Thought

Think about the people you have negotiated with or worked with. How would you describe them? What would you say their style was? What successful strategies have you found when dealing with them?

The Negotiation Framework

Earlier I introduced the idea that there were three high-level phases to the Negotiation Framework:

- Pre-Negotiation Planning
- Negotiating
- Reviewing

The following sections will look at each of these in more detail.

The Pre-Negotiation Planning Phase

To help in planning for the negotiation, it may be helpful to answer the following questions.

Question 1: What are the objectives?

You must have clear objectives before you go into the negotiation, otherwise you will just drift from discussion to discussion without a target to aim for.

What might the objectives of the counterparty be?

Having an understanding of what you think they might ultimately be after will help to put you into a good position from the start and will form a key part in the remainder of the planning process.

Let's say you are looking to get a new car. Your objective could simply be to get a new car. This may be obvious but by keeping it high-level and open like this, you will not close down any options. If you have an objective such as get a second-hand silver 4x4 from a private seller within 10 miles of your house, you may find it very difficult to meet that objective. So, pick an objective that will deliver what you are looking for without being too restrictive.

Question 2: What is my understanding of the Initial Scope of the deal?

Based on the objectives above, what do you think you will be negotiating about, what are the contents of your Toy Box?

Initial Scope

Can you identify the major needs and wants for both sides? Your side should be easy but, as with the objective, you need to try to put yourself on to the other side of the table and have your best guess at what you think theirs will be.

You don't need to worry about immediately validating these as you will do this partly during the remaining planning and partly during the opening phase of the negotiation. Are the items linked in any way?

It may be useful to scatter the items across a page rather than listing them, to make it easier to identify any links. If mind maps work for you, then use a mind map.

If we go back to the car example, the scope could be:

- Number of Doors
- Engine size
- Fuel type
- Transmission type
- Extras
- Servicing

Question 3: Who should be on my team and what is their role – and what about the counterparty?

Once you have an idea of what is going to be involved in the negotiation (the scope) then you can start to identify if you need help, who you need to help you and what their role should be. Your team.

Then you should turn your thoughts to who will be on the other side and if you can, what their primary negotiation style might be (Thinker, Controller, Pleaser or Energiser) as this will help you to prepare more effectively.

If we go back to the car example, it might be useful to have a mechanic with you to help you assess the car's condition beyond how it looks.

Question 4: Do I need to create a Foundation Package with Options?

If your negotiation has many moving parts or it is part of a competitive process, then you should look to create a Foundation Package.

This Foundation Package may contain items that are:

- Standard
- Satisfactory to both sides
- The minimum required

- Easy to understand

Then each of the other items become Options that can be added into the package if there appears to be a need or interest from your counterparty.

Again, with our car example, the Foundation Package could be the car with only the standard options, then things like air conditioning, heated seats, tinted windows may be the Options.

Question 5: Where do we think a deal can be achieved?

Given all the issues identified in either the Initial Scope or Foundation Package and Options, you need to complete the Target Calculator by identifying the following:

- Our Limit
- Their Estimated Limit
- Our Target
- Our Initial Position

If you have Options, then you need to do this for them as well.

Our Limit – This is the point beyond which you cannot go. It needs to be a position that the negotiator or the negotiation team can buy into and stick to. If not, there is a risk that you will do a deal that is beyond Our Limit. To work it out, consider what your BATNA, Best Alternative to a Negotiated Agreement is. This can be viewed as a list of alternatives to successfully completing the deal which is ranked in order of preference. Be careful that you are comparing like for like, as there may well be slight differences in either real or perceived value that need to be considered. One example of this is quality. If you have a higher-quality product, then you should factor this in when trying to create your BATNA. If you are in the situation that you have a very binary choice (either do it or don't do it) then you essentially don't have any alternatives, so your limit in this case needs to be agreed around the context of the negotiation as you understand it to be.

Their Estimated Limit – This is the point beyond which we think they will not go. Unless you have facts, this will just be an estimate – and if this is going to be the case, it is worth spending time researching it. As with Our Limit, you need to try to work out their BATNA by listing out all their alternatives and ranking them in the order in which you think they are likely to move through if they cannot get a deal with you. Again, don't forget to take into account real or perceived value when calculating this. The more time you can dedicate to researching, the better the position you will be able to take going into the negotiation.

Once we have these two items, we can identify the **Estimated Agreement Zone**. This is also known as the Zone of Possible Agreement or Realistic Settlement Zone. Essentially, this is the initial estimated gap between the two limits (theirs and ours) that we are going to have to plan to bridge in the negotiation.

Our Target – When going into a negotiation, hoping to get something out of it is like going into a cave to fetch a pot of gold from the back with only a single match for light. You have no idea how deep the cave is or for how long the match will burn. You are not sure when to strike the match and may well end up fumbling around in the dark until you find the pot. The one thing you do not want to do is to fumble around in the dark looking for something when you are negotiating, so give yourself a measurable and realistic target. For it to be realistic, it must lie within the Estimated Agreement Zone; for it to be measurable, you need to put a specific value against it. Finally, this is when we can start to become more ambitious in setting out what we are going to try to get. You spent time working out Their Estimated Limit based upon their alternatives to you, so why not use this as a framing point for your target. Set it at a point where you feel that, while it might take hard work to obtain it, it is still achievable. As a minimum, there should be around 75% of the

Estimated Agreement Zone between Our Target and Our Limit.

Our Initial Position – This is the last piece of this question to be answered and should be better (i.e. higher or lower) than Our Target but be careful how big you make the gap. If it is too big then you can run the risk of having real credibility issues, as the counterparty may not take you seriously. So just, in negotiation terms, nibble for a little bit more beyond Our Target and Their Estimated Limit. If you are working with numbers, then you could look to add between 15% and 25% of the Estimated Agreement Zone.

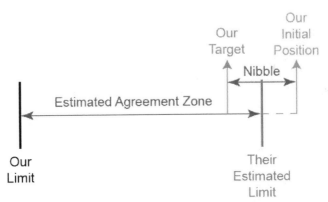

The Target Calculator

Back to the car...

You have found your ideal car and the price is currently £10,125.

You only have £10,000 available for this purchase so your limit, the most you can pay is £10,000.

At the other end of the scale you have no idea if the car seller has any other alternatives to you, but you reckon that they may be able to give a maximum of a 10% discount. This means that their estimated limit is £9,112.50.

This means that in this instance a deal is likely to be achieved between £10,000 and £9,112.50, the Estimated Agreement Zone.

Your target needs to be ambitious but realistic, so you are going to set that close to Their Estimated Limit, in this case £9,250, and to give you a chance to get this, you are going to nibble for a bit more with your Opening Position and start at £9,050.

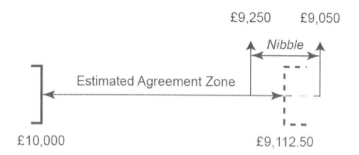

Question 6: What information do we want to get from them?

Before you can make any kind of offer in a negotiation, you need to try to get as much information from the counterparty as possible. Not only do you need to find out what they are expecting to be included in the package, you also need to try to understand their underlying wants, needs and desires.

You need to prepare a series of open questions that will get your counterparty talking.

You need to get a GRIP of the dialogue:

- **G**et it Going
- **R**eveal
- **I**nterests
- **P**osition

If we go back to our car example, a **G**et it going question could be, "Tell me about history of the car?" Based on the answer, a **R**eveal question could be "Does it have a full-service history?" or "Have you had many people looking at it?" Then an **I**nterests question could be "Would it be ready to take away today?" Finally, a **P**osition question could be "So if we can agree on a price, and if I can pay in cash and take it away today, could that work for you?" There is no commitment, but you might be able to gauge the value of the offer from the response.

These build into the Discovery Grid, along with the answers to questions 7 and 8.

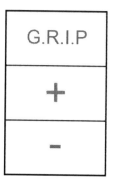

The Discovery Grid

Question 7: What positive information do we want to share with them?
Any information that you share with the other side must be positive at best and neutral at worst. It should look to build on the power you bring into the negotiation or to create power.

If you are preparing for a team negotiation, then you also need to prepare who is going to say what. This will help to ensure that there is no confusion during the negotiation.

For our car example, letting them know we have cash could be good or that you are able to move quickly could also be beneficial to help get the price lowered.

Question 8: What negative information do we not want to share with them?

Anything that either destroys value or reduces your position of power in a negotiation should be avoided, so make a note of this – especially if you are negotiating in a team.

With the car, you wouldn't want to tell the seller the maximum amount you are prepared to pay or that you really need a car.

Question 9: What are we looking to trade?

Concessions in a negotiation fall into one of three categories:

- **Negotiables** – What are you prepared to negotiate to get the deal you are looking for.
- **Wants** – This is what you want to get in return for the item you are prepared to negotiate. There should be at least one item in here for each item in the Negotiable box.
- **Non-negotiables** – These are the concessions that you do not want to trade. This category

will contain items such as those that you are not authorised to trade or those that will take you from Our Target to Our Limit.

Negotiables
Wants
Non-Negotiables

The Trader's Grid

It is worth pointing out that if one of your Non-negotiables is asked for, then you may need take an adjournment to plan what you are going to do.

With the car, if you were buying it from a dealer rather than privately, you might be prepared to increase your offer if the seller was to include servicing. The Negotiable could be "+£100" and the associated Want could be "3 Year's Servicing". A Non-

Negotiable could be "Full mechanical safety check before delivery".

Question 10: What are we going to say to kick off the negotiation?
This is the Move to Business Statement that will be delivered as the meeting moves from introductions and social chit-chat into business.

This is your opportunity to set the scene and get the attention of the counterparty.

This Move to Business Statement has three main sections:

- **Transition statement** – Thank you very much for coming in. We have a great opportunity ahead of us...
- **Power Card** – As I am sure you are aware, we are looking at a number of options...
- **Expectation** – If we can reach an agreement today then...

This statement must be short, relevant and – above all – planned.

As a final example with our car purchase, "Hi, I see you have a few great cars out there, but there is one that I am interested in... I have been looking around a few dealers and have seen the same car a couple of times for a similar price... I am not going to mess you around and go back to the other dealers but if we can agree on a good price, I am prepared do a deal with you..."

The Negotiating Phase

The negotiating phase of the framework contains five steps that should be taken in order. The Expert Negotiator's five steps to success are:

- Opening Phase
  - Step 1 - Scene Setting
  - Step 2 - Discovery
  - Step 3 - Positioning
- Trading Phase
  - Step 4 - Trading
- Closing Phase
  - Step 5 – Closing

The first three steps make up the Opening Phase of the negotiation and, because they are more about information than bargaining, they are often viewed as not being part of the negotiation. But as we will see, these are probably the most important steps of the negotiation – and if you get them right, the remaining steps/phases, Trading and Closing, often fall into place relatively easily.

Step 1: Scene Setting

Introductions

The first step in any meeting is the introductions. As a negotiator, these take on additional significance. They allow you to:

- Confirm attendees
- Check authority/seniority in the room

Building Relationships

This initial exchange allows you to start to build a relationship with the counterparty and can give you an insight into:

- Their negotiation style
- Their attitude towards you
- Any deadlines or other potential sources of power for you

For example, you could ask about summer holidays, where they are going, how long they will be away for and when they are going. The amount of conversation you get may tell you how open they are going to be or potentially what their style is. It may also give you a date by which the deal should be completed.

Move to Business

There will come a time when you will move from introductions to business. This is when you get the opportunity to deliver your Move to Business Statement you prepared during Pre-Negotiation Planning. Once you have finished, give the counterparty the chance to deliver their own Move to Business statement. They may not have one, but if you continue to talk for too long, they will start to switch off – or worse, they will start to feel that you have no interest in them and begin to put up barriers.

Step 2: Discovery

Build the Scope of the Negotiation

Using the Initial Scope or Foundation Package, build the scope along with your counterparty. You should grasp the opportunity to take the lead by using a flip chart or a whiteboard or a sheet of paper and start to draw up the scope. Once you have put all your items on the board, ask your counterparty if there is anything they would like to add.

Finally, once the creation of the scope has been completed and all items confirmed, check that it is possible to reach agreement on all the items. If not, it might be worth either trying to get the additional decision makers into the room or identifying the items on which it is possible to reach agreement. As a last resort, it may be necessary to take a break at this stage to regroup.

Ask Questions

Try to get the counterparty talking first about the package. Use the GRIP questions (part of the Discovery Grid) that you have planned, starting with any items that they may have added.

It is up to you to discover the counterparty's interests, as they are unlikely to openly tell you them, and there can be problems with this. Their interests could be compared to an iceberg, in that most of them will be undeclared. In fact, they can be more interested in putting their position out there than discussing why things are important to them. But persist by asking open questions and making constructive comments that lead them to open up.

Giving Information

Using the Positives box in the Discovery Grid as your guide, start to share information with the other side that is related to the items on the Scope of the Negotiation.

Step 3: Positioning

Preparing

During planning, you worked out what Our Initial Position will be based on what you understood the Scope of the Negotiation to be, but...

- Has this Scope changed?
- Have you been given any new information that you had not considered before?
- Have you been given information that either weakens or strengthens your power?
- Is there a different perception of value?
- Is there anything that I can now bring in from the outside?

If the answer to any of these questions is "yes" then you need to revisit planning and assess your Initial Position, as carrying on may result in a bad deal for both sides.

Delivering

Once you are happy with your planning and the validity of your Initial Position, you need to deliver it with conviction. You are essentially setting an anchor and indicating that it is going to be very hard for the counterparty to get you to move away from it.

To do this, follow these three steps:

1. Summarise the Scope of the Negotiation
2. Deliver your position without using loose language
3. Shut up

This could be something like:

"Given that we are going to be providing 234 widgets by 31st December via airfreight to your warehouse at Aberdeen Airport, and you are going to pay us on 31st January by bank transfer, the total price for this order inclusive of VAT is £34,678."

From this statement it is very clear what is being ordered, when it will be delivered, when we will be paid and how much it will cost. It contains no loose language.

Loose language covers phrases that can indicate that you are not really too sure about your positions such as:

- We were hoping for...
- I'd/we would like...
- My opening offer is...
- We were looking for 22?
- Our offer is in the range of 34–44
- We could do it for 78
- How about 220?

Finally, support what you are saying with how you are saying it. Don't look embarrassed or shifty; sit up straight and look them in the eye. In other words, look as if you mean it, as if you have thought long and hard about your position and have not just plucked it out of the air.

Responding

Once you hear an opening position from the counterparty, remembering that they may not phrase it as clearly as you will, you need to respond with an indication that it is not good enough. This is known as The Flinch. It is a power play technique which, if used correctly, can put pressure on the counterparty.

A flinch is often a natural reaction when we hurt ourselves or when we see something we don't like. It is a way of showing that we are not very happy with the current situation, and therefore we should flinch when we hear or receive a position from a counterparty.

The flinch should be noticeable so don't just shake your head. You could use silence to reinforce the act but tell them that that just won't work, and why, but remember this is not to be a personal insult – keep it professional and about the deal.

The last thing about flinching is that you should *always* do it – even if you like the position you have been given. You need to do this for two reasons. Firstly, you are using it as a power play, and you may get them to move. Remember that the first position that people put on the table will rarely be their best, so push back. Secondly, if you accept the first offer, you may appear too eager and leave them wondering what they got wrong. This may result in more niggling and pushback during the following phases as they try to recoup some of the perceived lost value.

Step 4: Trading

Trading is all about getting the counterparty to move towards you by getting what you need and giving only what you want. You need to be reflecting to the counterparty that as time goes by in the trading process, you are running out of items to trade – so much so that they get the impression that you are getting close to your limit. In reality, you are getting close to your target because whatever we plan to trade has to be designed to take you from Our Initial Position to Our Target.

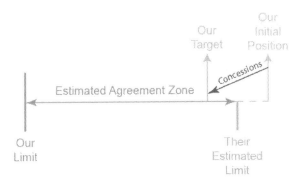

The Purpose of Trading

Everything that takes us from Our Target to Our Limit initially sits under the Untradeable category but may come into play after the Opening Phase.

The people who are often best at this, or who appear to be best, are market traders – and they have a number of rules by which they abide

.

Tips for Trading

While the following suggestions are not exhaustive, they will put you into a better position during trading and make it easier for you to resist tricks and tactics:

- Plan your concessions
  - o Use the Trader's Grid during planning.

- Be prepared to walk away
  - o The power of a full and final offer can be great; just be careful how and when you use it because if you make the threat, you need to be prepared to follow through.

- Send and respond to signals
  - o If you want to show excitement then show it; similarly, if you want to show frustration then show it – just don't make it personal.
  - o If you are reading excitement or frustration from the other side, then respond to it; remember that you want

to maintain the momentum you have built up.

  o If they start to talk about next steps, don't continue to trade – try to close.

- Have room to move
  o Always be thinking, planning and – if necessary – adjusting. You may need to adjust your Initial Position based on changes to the package.
  o If you don't have room to move, then you need to be prepared to move away.

- Never give anything away for free
  o You are trading, not compromising or accommodating. For everything you are going to give, make sure you get something in return.

- All concessions are conditional
  o This is how we make sure we get something in return. Every concession you give must have a condition attached to it. That way if they don't accept the condition, then they don't get the concession.

- Flinch
  - Once again, don't make it too easy for them. Flinch to show that their offer is just not good enough.

- Be patient
  - Watch time deadlines, as these can play against you in this instance. You need to try to give yourself enough time to be patient.
  - Don't rush into trading concessions. It is very easy to get wrapped up in the excitement and be forced into giving something you didn't want to give.
  - Be prepared to give them time to consider, in silence. Don't allow this silence to bully you into movement.

- Package options
  - Do not allow yourself to become restricted to talking about individual items. Try to keep everything as a package.
  - The trick is to try to keep as many of the package items as possible under discussion, potentially indicating that they are related.

- o Try to avoid giving multiple concessions at once. Always work to build them in one at a time.

- Reflect interests/needs
  - o Being able to trade in a way that seems to tick all the boxes of the other side is what often sets the skilled trader apart.
  - o In the opening phase, you should have taken time to understand the needs, wants and interests of the counterparty. Use this information to help you plan the order in which you are going to trade your concessions. You may be able to trade something that means very little to you but means a lot to them. This has the potential to create a result where the value for both parties has, or is perceived to have, increased.
  - o Plan the order in which you trade concessions so that the value of each item appears to be getting smaller. This can indicate to the counterparty that you are running out of items to trade. This will be true as we approach Our Limit or may be perceived as true as we approach Our Target.

Step 5: Closing

The biggest challenge for most negotiators is not necessarily when to close or how to close because there tends to come a point in the negotiation when everyone kind of runs out of things to say or do and so they stumble into the close. A good negotiator recognises when to close (so that they get the best possible deal) and how to close (so that they minimise the risk of conflict going forward).

When to Close

We have identified that observation is one of the key tasks of The Expert Negotiator, and this is no different in closing. You need to be listening for what the counterparty says, watching their behaviour and understanding the difference in position, to be able to identify if there is an opportunity to close the negotiation. Some of the indicators are:

- Positions are close
  - When the gap between both sides appears to be quite small, don't point out the gap – point out the closeness and try to close the negotiation.

- They ask "what next" questions
  - They might start to ask implementation-type questions, which can indicate that – in their minds at least – everything is OK with the terms and conditions of the negotiation. If you agree, get them to close before moving on.

- They are sending signals
  - For example, they may start to get excited or enthusiastic in the way they are talking.
  - Their posture may appear more relaxed or they may lean forward in expectation.
  - They may simply tell you what they can agree to.

- A deadline is approaching
  - Deadlines create pressure. You may be able to turn this pressure to your advantage if the deadline is on their side.

- We have reached Our Target
    - The whole reason for having a target is to give you something to try to get to, so why not try to close once you get to that point.

- We have reached Our Limit
    - Finally, this is when you have to reach agreement or be prepared to walk away, either with no deal or in deadlock.

How to Close

Once you have recognised that the time is right to close, you need to do it, and while there are a number of different ways to close – which we will look at later – there are a few guidelines for closing:

1. Don't add in anything new – There can be a temptation to try to slip something in here at the last minute, but don't as this will not help the relationship.

2. Summarise – Don't assume that everybody has the same understanding as you, so summarise what has been agreed and be specific. Don't say that delivery will be at the end of October; say delivery will be on 31st October. Don't say that the total fee is 35k; say that the total fee is £35k.

3. Get the Agreement – This does not have to be a fully signed contract at this stage but get them to commit to making the agreement with you.

4. Close the meeting and stop talking about it – If it has been a tough or tense negotiation, there is a risk once the pressure is off that

someone may say something about the deal that can cause problems.

Closing Techniques and Counters

There are many different ways to "close" the deal or get agreement. Below are some of these which I have found work well.

Give an Alternative

Give the counterparty just one other option, but make sure that both options work for you. You don't want to risk them choosing an option that is worse for you.

For example, "We have two options: Option 1, without the special widget, is £345; Option 2, with the special widget, is £456."

If someone tries that with you then you could counter the close by taking one that works for you and flinch at it.

For example, "Thanks, Option 1 is good, but I am afraid that the reduction in price isn't quite going to be enough."

Use a Concession

You may need to trade a concession to get the close. This is probably not going to be a Matched Trade from the Trader's Grid, so you may need to take a little bit of time to work though the implications of the trade.

For example, "If you will agree to the deal then we will give you widget W."

If someone tries that with you then you could counter the close by taking the concession and flinching.

For example, "Thanks, but I am afraid that widget W is just not quite enough. If you give us widgets W and D then we have an agreement."

The Puppy Dog

Are you able to give them a trial? If so, make sure to put your best foot forward in the pilot.

For example, "Tell you what, before we go any further, why don't you give it a go for a few weeks?"

If someone tries that with you then you could counter the close by not accepting the trial without agreeing the final terms.

For example, "Thanks, but I would prefer to have an agreement in place first."

Be Assumptive

Talk about the next steps, delivery options, support arrangements, etc., making the actual deal appear to have been concluded.

For example, "I can deliver the report on Friday. Would you like it emailed or printed and then scanned?"

If someone tries that with you then you could counter the close by flinching and going back to the deal under negotiation.

For example, "Thanks, but Friday is too late – we need to have the report sooner. Can you deliver it on Thursday?"

Use an Adjournment

Summarise the current deal, get them to think about the agreement, and set a time to get back together.

For example, "Given where we have got to, the offer on the table is £45,323. We will give you until Friday at 5pm to think about it."

If someone tries that with you then you could counter the close by not letting them walk out without something to think about, essentially a condition.

For example, "OK, and while you are out can you think about your fee, as that is not something we can agree on."

Then when you get back together...

"So, have you had a chance to reconsider your fee? If you can come down just a little, then I think we can reach an agreement."

Give a Full and Final
If you are going to do this, you need to mean it – otherwise you will become the weakest party around the table.

For example, "For widgets X, Y and Z, our full and final offer for 7000 units is £430,700."

If someone tries that with you then you could counter the close by flinching and seeing if they mean it. If they do, then you either take it or leave it.

For example, "I'm sorry, but that just does not work for us. We are close, but just not there yet."

Adjournments

Adjournments can be either planned (for example, the agreed end of the meeting) or they can be tactical (for example, when something unexpected or unplanned happens and you need to take a break to plan your next steps). Either way, you should follow the same basic procedure.

Before Adjourning

Before you leave the room, you need to:

- Summarise the current situation
  - You should not make assumptions about the counterparty's understanding of the deal.
  - This is also an opportunity to validate your understanding.

- Tell them what you are going to do
  - Be honest – tell them what you are going to do, but just don't make any promises.

- Give them something to do
  - If not, they will probably spend time trying to second guess you.

o If you are going to make a concession, then what are you going to trade for it? Get them to think about the condition. For example, if you are happy to make a price reduction if you can get better payment terms then make sure you get the counterparty to think about their options for payment terms.

- Tell them how long the adjournment will be
  o Unless you want to put pressure on them, be realistic about the time required.

- Get up and go
  o Don't start discussing anything else.
  o If you are a team, then no one in the team should start talking about anything else.

During the Adjournment

While you are out of the room, plan. Use your notes as a starting point and work through all the options that are available to you. Bring other people in to help you, if necessary, but use the time to plan what you are going to do when you go back in.

As an aside, be careful that you are not being spied on. You may think that no one would ever do such a thing in your negotiations, but some people will do anything to gain an advantage.

After the Adjournment
When you come back into the meeting, you need to:

- Summarise the situation when you left
  - Before moving on, make sure that everybody agrees where you left off.

- Ask them where they are at on the matter you gave them to discuss
  - Getting them talking first can show that you are willing to have a discussion rather than impose positions.
  - Also, you might find that you don't need to move.

- Be firm on your position.
  - If you are not firm, then there was no real need for the adjournment; remember that you can still make changes using the package.

The Reviewing Phase

Regardless of the result of the negotiation, you must carry out some form of review. The level of detail in the review will be defined by the amount of time that is allocated to it, which will be determined by the importance you place on the task.

The more time you allocate the better, as this review should also become part of your input into subsequent negotiations and perhaps even provide an indication as to areas where additional assistance may be required.

How to Review

Someone needs to take control of the review process and, given that we take a role-based approach to tasks, this is the responsibility of the Manager.

If it has been a solo negotiation, then it is down to the solo negotiator, as they will have fulfilled all roles, and so they are responsible for both managing and performing the review.

If it has been a team negotiation, then the person who performed the role of Manager is responsible for organising both the review meeting and the attendees. In this case, the attendees should include anybody who has been involved in both the pre-negotiation planning and the negotiation. It is not a place to bring in "outsiders," as there needs to be complete openness. The Observer will have a major input into the process as their notes will be a significant source of information.

When it comes to the review meeting, there are just two categories that you need to use during the negotiation:

- **What was good** – under this, note down everything that went to plan, was successfully executed, performed as expected, etc.
- **What could have been better** – under this, note down everything that didn't reach expectations, underperformed, failed, etc.

Finally, use the output to build on the good stuff and work towards eliminating the others.

What to Review

This is not a witch-hunt! This an opportunity to understand what should be repeated or may be required to be modified to get the best possible result in future negotiations.

Any feedback must be:

- **Specific** – provide examples. Don't simply say, "Our communication was good"; provide specific examples.

- **Constructive** – don't just criticise, offer suggestions.
- **Timely** – give it while it is fresh and relevant. There is no point in giving feedback six months after the event.

Use the following headings as a guide for your review:

- Relationships
- Process
- Environment

Relationships

Look at the relationship between you and the counterparty and try to identify the areas that worked well and if there was anything that could have been done better to create and/or maintain a good relationship.

Look at specifics such as:

- any areas of conflict
- personality clashes

Also think about:

- how you communicated – when you spoke, was it firm and with conviction?
- did you listen to what they were saying?
- did you pick up on their body language?

- did your body language reflect and support what you were saying?
- were you able to identify their style?
- was the counterparty as expected?

If it was a team negotiation:

- did the team function?
- did the members stay within their assigned roles?
- were you able to identify weaknesses in their team?

Process

Given the guidelines for planning and the frameworks for negotiating, where did you do well and where could you have been better?

Consider areas such as:

- were there any surprises in the package?
- were there clearly identifiable objectives?
- were we prepared for discovery?
- the quality of the notes
- the control of the process from pre-negotiation planning to the negotiation to this review
- the actual outcome achieved compared with the planned outcome

Also look at:

- did we complete all the tasks in a step?
- did we match our concessions to their interests?
- did we use adjournments effectively?

Environment

This part of the review should cover what was good about the administration, facilities, equipment and materials as well as where these could have been better.

Look at specifics such as:

- the room or call set-up
- the materials
- administration and logistics

Also think about:

- Refreshments
- Breakout areas
- Initial meet and greet
- Use of technology

Key Takeaways

The Three Phases of the Negotiation Framework:

- Pre-Negotiation Planning
  - ○ Objectives
  - ○ Initial Scope
  - ○ Our roles and their styles
  - ○ Foundation package and options
  - ○ The Target Calculator
  - ○ The Discovery Grid
  - ○ The Trader's Grid
  - ○ The Power Statement
- Negotiating
  - ○ Step 1 – Scene Setting
  - ○ Step 2 – Discovery
  - ○ Step 3 – Positioning
  - ○ Step 4 – Trading
  - ○ Step 5 - Closing
- Reviewing
  - ○ What did you do well and what could you have done better?

Further Thought

While this section may make a negotiation appear rigid, flexibility still needs to be applied. Reflect on past negotiations and identify where flexibility or creativity has helped and how you could slot those experiences into this framework.

Power Plays

These Power Plays are also referred to as gambits and in negotiation terms, the definition of a gambit is an action – typically entailing a degree of risk – which is calculated to gain an advantage.

The following sections group the power plays into the phases in which they are likely to appear, but they can be used at any stage. A good negotiator not only recognises each gambit and knows a countermeasure to test it, but also knows which have a chance of working given themselves, the negotiation and the other people involved.

Opening Phase Power Plays

As a reminder, the Opening Phase consists of the Scene Setting, Discovery and Positioning steps.

Padding

This is where non-essential issues are added to the package alongside real issues.

It works by providing trading room and can also reduce others' aspirations.

Countermeasure – Identify the items and question their validity or create your own padding and make sweeping trades.

Good Cop–Bad Cop

In this power play, one person plays "bad" by being threatening or aggressive or difficult, so other seems "nice" and more reasonable.

It works because the good cop engenders trust, lowers defences and makes it easier to make concessions to them.

Countermeasure – Focus on your original goals and objectives. Talk to the good guy, ignoring the bad cop or play hard with both.

Too Good to be True

Here, important information is left where you can conveniently find it.

It works by revealing a "false" position that then means a repositioning can take place without raising suspicions.

Countermeasure – if it seems too good to be true, it probably is. Test it.

Low Ball

With a Low Ball, they lure you into deal by offering a low price, get you hooked, and then add costs.

It works by building commitment to the deal and providing reasons for why you want it.

Countermeasure – Know what you want and ask for the price in full. Question the deal and, if necessary, walk away.

High Ball

Unlike the Low Ball, the High Ball lures you into deal with high compensation, get you hooked, and then offer is deflated.

It works by luring you into the deal with high incentives.

Countermeasure – If it feels too good, get the details of the deal in writing before committing.

Vice

The vice is used to force you to make a counter-offer, e.g. "You can do better than that."

It works by making you feel compelled to comply.

Countermeasure – Express the deal in a different way to point out what it contains and, if necessary, try to pin them down by "How much better?" or "Compared to what?"

Sunk Costs
This is where historical negotiations or relationships are used to influence the current negotiation.

It works because people feel a commitment to repeating what has already been done or they want to fix errors in the past.

Countermeasure – Ignore all past negotiations. This is a new deal and as such, a different deal.

Feared Experts
People can be intimidated by those who act with confidence or have an appearance of authority.

It works by making people question their own ability and knowledge.

Countermeasure – Don't confuse status, wealth, power or fame with their content expertise and its relevance to the negotiation.

Flattery

Something complementary is said to the other party.

It works because it is hard to dislike people who like you, and it lowers the other party's suspicions.

Countermeasure – Beware of compliments and don't allow them to impact your decision-making.

This is All I've Got

"I love your proposal, but I only have $1000." The other responds by changing proposal or showing alternatives available.

It works because of the negotiator's ego – everyone likes a compliment. By telling them you love their proposal, they may meet your budget to keep the good feelings flowing.

Countermeasure – Test the premise of the budget, as they could be flexible. Maybe different schedules of payment can be made, or you can change the package to fit the budget.

Trading Phase Power Plays

The Smart Dummy

Being slow to understand can lead to more concessions.

It works by leading impatient people to make unilateral concessions.

Countermeasure – Stick to your planning and don't change your package to "simplify it." Suggest they take time to understand or ask what additional information might help.

Funny Money

Changing the format of the offer, for example using percentages or monthly payments or a different currency.

It works because we sometimes find alternative forms of money easier to spend.

Countermeasure – Take it back to what you understand and think in terms of real profit, real margins, real targets, real limits.

Limited Authority
They cannot make the decision stating that they must report to a higher authority.

It works by getting you to make concessions to person 1 and further concessions to person 2 and can ultimately wear you down.

Countermeasure – Check for authority first and make any agreements conditional. As a last resort, threaten to reopen the entire deal.

I Will if You Will
Something is given, and it is strongly suggested that the other owes something in return.

It works by making you feel guilty and, as a result, obliged to respond in kind.

Countermeasure – Don't accept it or give something inconsequential in return.

Hard to Get
Makes the counterparty work hard for any agreement with slow concessions.

It works because people get frustrated and it is easier to accept the deal as they place greater value on things that are hard to get.

Countermeasure – Stick to your planning and play the game back by taking your time to understand.

Hostage Tactic

If you don't meet our demands, then you won't get what I am holding.

It uses the fear of losing something to make you concede.

Countermeasure – Stick to your planning and look to get your own hostage based on what is important to them and offer to trade hostages. Point out the consequences to the deal if they continue to hold onto the hostage.

Silence and Bracketing

This calls attention to a certain part of the negotiation by mentioning it and then keeping silent.

It works by first focusing on important issues and then the silence makes it feel uncomfortable which can lead to unilateral concessions.

Countermeasure – Push back by probing their needs and asking what they want or why they are focusing on a specific item.

The Angry One

The counterparty acts angry over particular items in a deal.

It works because anger can intimidate and may make the counterparty think that you are close to your bottom line. As a result, there is a want to end quickly to avoid further anger.

Countermeasure – Take a break or table the discussion until the counterparty can control their anger. Offer to put anger as an item to negotiate. Acknowledge their anger, ask for examples and how they would like it to be rectified.

Turning the Tables

They ask you to argue their position, "If you were in our shoes, why would you accept it."

It works by shaking your confidence, and by putting you under pressure, it can undermine your argument.

Countermeasure – Be confident in your preparation and explain why the deal is good. Take time to compose yourself and put things into perspective.

Scarcity
Makes any negotiated item seem very difficult to get.

It works by making them believe that what you have is difficult for them to get. This relies on a belief that items that are difficult to get are typically better than those that are easy to possess.

Countermeasure – Stick to your planning, take your time and if necessary, carry out additional research to understand the true value and availability of the item being offered.

False Comparisons
Comparisons are made between the current offer and the initial offer which was miss-represented in the first place.

It works by making the counterparty feel like they are now getting good value by comparison.

Countermeasure – Ignore the initial offer and take your time to assess the current offer based on the situation.

Closing Phase Power Plays

Nibbling

Adding on a last-minute item right before striking a deal.

It works when the counterparty is tired or up against a time constraint or does not want to risk losing the main deal.

Countermeasure – Suggest that the additional item is traded into the deal, ask if there is anything else or threaten to reopen the entire deal.

Puppy Dog

This gets you hooked into a product or service by allowing you to try it before paying for it.

It works because as you get used to using something you build a commitment to it, and you will give yourself reasons as to why you need to keep it.

Countermeasure – Don't accept it unless the terms of the deal are all agreed, and you know exactly what you are getting.

Ultimatum

This is a take it or leave it play and can force you to accept or reject offer.

It works by making you think that the counterparty can do no better.

Countermeasure – Question why they are giving you an ultimatum and be prepared to walk away. Help the counterparty back down by giving them a way out by creating new alternatives.

Time Deadlines

Imposing time constraints which can lead to quick and large concessions.

It works by making you feel the need to seal the deal even if it's not satisfactory.

Countermeasure – Question the deadline and offer to work towards it. Know your limits and work towards those.

Bait and Switch

You are sold X and on delivery it is switched to Y.

It works because you make a psychological commitment to make a purchase and find it hard to pull out, even with the changes.

Countermeasure – Ask why the switch has occurred and, if necessary, walk away.

Key Takeaways

- Powerplays are often used in a negotiation and are designed to create an edge.
- Sometimes they are real but other times they are being used with no substance.
- Test everything.
- Trust your planning.
- Take your time and don't allow yourself to be forced into a bad decision.
- Use the one that will work for you and the current situation.

Further Thought

Are you comfortable playing games or bluffing during a negotiation? If not, then there is not much point in you trying to use a Power Play as a bluff. You will struggle to deliver it effectively and you will find it even harder to defend it if challenged. Look for valid sources of power and use them instead. Unfortunately, you may also struggle to call out a bluffer as there may be a fear of conflict. If you feel you are being bluffed, you must not let it impact you and your decision making. Look at the countermeasures identified in this section and work out a way for you to use them in a way you are comfortable with.

Body Language

As we are talking about negotiation rather than dating, there are only a few signs that you need to look out for:

- Lying
- Frustration
- Rejection
- Acceptance

If you spot any of the following signs, don't make assumptions about them – test them.

Lying

This is the tell-tale sign that is most often looked for in negotiation, but it is also the most difficult because there is no single sign that can be definitely tied to lying. Many of the signs are brought on by anxiety, embarrassment, adrenaline or fear, so there is no guarantee that the counterparty is lying.

Some of the signs of lying are:

- Covering the mouth – children do this. It is almost as if they are trying to catch or stop the lie as it comes out of their mouth.
- Scratching the upper lip or nose – again this is about covering up the mouth.

- Uncontrolled blushing – this can be a physiological response to anxiety.
- Facing the palms downwards – this change of hand gestures can indicate that the body is tensing up.
- Lip licking – anxiety releases adrenalin, which can cause our mouths and throats to dry up.
- Sudden crossing of the legs – becoming defensive, almost waiting to be found out.
- Sudden crossing of the arms – becoming defensive, almost waiting to be found out.
- Glancing away/sideways – this is something we do when we are embarrassed.
- Forced eye contact – in trying to deflect the glance, eye contact becomes false.
- Overly stiff posture – the anxiety caused by lying can result in a tensing of muscles.
- Fidgeting – trying to get comfortable in an uncomfortable situation.
- Hand hiding – trying to counter the change in gestures by hiding their hands.
- Stutters, slurs and hesitations – it's not always easy to tell a lie!
- Sweating and palm wiping – pretty extreme, but again this is a reaction to the anxiety.
- Sudden giggling – this, again, can be a nervous reaction to stress.

These tend to be triggered by anxiety, so they may not happen immediately and may be encouraged by silence. If you think there may have been a lie, count to 10 before responding – and watch. Also, ask questions to test; see if you get an overly detailed response.

While this is a fairly comprehensive list, the key to recognising lying is to interpret the signs correctly and compare them to what you have observed as normal behaviour – especially during Scene Setting, as this tends to be the most relaxed step in the Negotiation.

After working with one of my clients, they went into a contract negotiation with a key supplier. During planning they admitted to me that they really needed this provider, but they also needed to bring back a good deal. Already my client was feeling on the back foot. After a couple of meetings, I met up with them just after they had received an offer and noticed a change in attitude. Their confidence was up, and they felt on top of the negotiation. I asked them what had changed, and they told me they had spotted a lie and challenged them. The supplier told them that this was a take it or leave it opportunity, they obviously felt confident, and my client simply said nothing, stared back and started to shake their heads. As they did this the supplier licked their lips, swallowed deeply and squirmed in their chair. My client noticed this and after another brief pause said "Really, do you not want this contract?" At that the supplier hesitated and said, "Well I think we can find some common ground here" and told my client they would go away and see what they could do. The supplier then came back with an offer that was 10% better and they were looking forward to moving forward.

Frustration

There is some crossover between frustration and anxiety when it comes to body language, but – as with lying – look at the body language in the context of the person, situation and verbal communication.

If they are rubbing the back of their head while tapping the table with their palms facing down after you explained the same thing for the 10th time, it is probably not a lie but frustration.

Some of the signs of frustration are:

- Scratching the back of the head
- Rubbing the back of the neck
- Shaking the head repeatedly
- Tapping the table repeatedly
- Rubbing the face firmly
- Looking away while shaking the head
- Making/clenching a fist
- Deep breaths/sighing

These signs may be the initial steps towards deadlock, so watch for them and try to change direction; become creative or get them talking to regain the momentum.

Frustration can be difficult to pick up early in the negotiation as the signs can be more subtle, but if you can identify it quickly, you can turn a potentially difficult situation around. I had one such situation where a colleague was taking the client through the details behind our proposal and about forty-five minutes into the meeting I started to notice that two of the client team were starting to show signs of frustration. One was drumming their fingers on the table and the other was rubbing their neck and shaking their heads. My colleague had just taken a breath and I decided to do something I don't often do and said "Pete, can we just pause for a minute?" Everybody in the room looked at me and for a brief second there was a quizzical atmosphere. I then asked Jane, the client who was drumming her fingers, what she had heard so far that she liked, and she said nothing. That could have been the end of the meeting, but I then asked what she was looking to hear, and she told me. I then asked the same question of Simon, who had been shaking his head, and he told me that he too was waiting to hear the same thing as Jane. I then checked with the rest of the room if there were any questions and if they were happy to move on. They were, so we did. It was a risky move but sometimes, when you spot that things are not going well, you need to take a few risks to keep things moving forward.

Rejection

This can come as part of a flinch, but it can also come separately.

Some of the signs of rejection are:

- Looking away
- Arms crossed
- Head shaking
- Eye rubbing
- Lip pursing

If it is done in silence, then allow the silence to remain and start to ask questions to help you understand what is causing the rejection. See if you can deal with them without a change in your position.

I had one counterparty who overplayed rejection. They groaned very loudly while at the same time they rubbed their eyes and shook their head. I immediately stopped talking and looked at them with my eyebrows furrowed in what could be described as a quizzical look. They made eye contact, and I could tell that they were not really rejecting what I was saying, they had no answer to my challenge. This should serve as a warning that if you are going to try to use body language to reinforce what you are saying, make sure you can back up your body language.

Acceptance

Finally, you want to recognise possible acceptance. Recognising the signs of potential acceptance can be an indication to move to step 5 and try to close the deal.

Some of the signs of acceptance are:

- Nodding
- Eyebrow raises
- Leaning forward
- Quick look up

My final example in this section on body language comes from some of the training I do. When we use video review of simulated negotiations, I am more often than not able to point out the moment an offer has been accepted. Without fail, there is a quick look up or an eyebrow raise followed by a very brief nod or smile. The simulation may progress for another 10 or 15 minutes but it tends to revolve around minor details and the outcome is very close to that initially accepted offer.

Key Takeaways

- You must be looking at someone to assess their body language; use the Observer role to do this in a team setting.
- Be very careful when assessing; it can be very easy to misinterpret.
- Look at what people are saying as well as their body language.
- Don't focus your efforts on trying to identify the negatives, look for and react to the positives as well.
- Remember your own body language; is it saying what you want it to say?
- Use it to reinforce what you are saying; if you are excited, look excited.

Further Thought

Knowing how people are lying is the most common area of interest for body language, but as I have said a few times already, be very careful when making any assessments. There is a very good book, Spy the Lie (Don Tennant, Michael Floyd, and Susan Carnicero), which looks at this very subject. It looks at it from the perspective of interrogations, but the same basic principles can be applied to negotiations for spotting and reacting to lies.

Dealing with Deadlock

Deadlock in negotiations is either real or another form of gambit, so the first thing you should do is to test the gambit and see if you can work around it.

Restate and Shut Up

I am not suggesting that you just repeat the stumbling block parrot fashion and see what happens. Rather you should look to reframe it in a way that is designed to get them talking and then to keep them talking as much as possible, trying to minimise the impact of the issue as you attempt to move forward out of deadlock.

Change the Location

The negotiations up to this point may have been taking place at a specific location, and it may be that coming back to the same location is becoming a problem. Changing the location may mean that all the old assumptions about what would or would not work are (almost) thrown out the window. This fresh perspective might be just what both sides need to go back and revisit the issue that is causing the deadlock.

Change the Negotiator

We can be so afraid of failure that we almost never consider this possibility, but it can be a powerful option. Sometimes we run into a deadlock because one or more of the negotiators is no longer able either to separate the deal from the people or to see any other way around the current situation. This is more likely to be the case if the negotiations have been going on for a long time. If you change the negotiator then you may find that the relationship and trust-building element of the negotiation has to start again, but this delay might be worth it. Indeed, it might be just what is needed to move the discussions forward out of deadlock.

Bring in a Mediator/Arbitrator/The Boss

Often a deadlock is a result of the negotiating parties not having the authority needed to be able to suggest an alternative. If this is the case, then a good way to deal with the problem is to pass it up to a higher authority. They may be able to quickly find areas in which they can bend, and that could get the whole discussion back on track quickly. If that is not the case or the negotiation is still in deadlock, then bringing in an independent third party to either mediate or arbitrate can be useful.

Point out the Consequences to All

Each side of the table must have a reason for not being willing to budge on the deadlock issue. This reason is based on the information that they currently have. Sometimes bringing the information upon which you have based your position and presenting it in a way that points out the consequences to both sides of not completing the deal might help to get things moving. The other side might point out that one of your assumptions is incorrect, or they may be surprised to learn a fact that they didn't know about. Either way, this might be just what is needed to get things moving again.

Have an "Off the Record" Conversation

Depending on the level of rapport that you have been able to build with the other side, this might be an option. When you go "off the record," you indicate to the other side that whatever you say to each other must and will remain "off the record" and will not be mentioned again. This is designed to show how much you trust the other side and to see if perhaps both sides of the table are trying to reach the same end and are just getting tripped up by a minor issue.

Change the Package

Although this doesn't really mean anything by itself, it's a great way to communicate to the other side that you would like to find a way to create a solution that works for both sides. Just by indicating that this is what you are working towards can often be the spark that causes the other side to start to consider more possible ways around your deadlock.

Take an Adjournment

It sounds so simple that often we overlook it but taking a break and stepping away from the table can often be the most powerful way to break a negotiation deadlock. We all tend to get caught up in a negotiation when we are in the thick of it, and our ability to think of creative ways to resolve deadlocks can decrease the longer that we've been negotiating. But remember to set a time to come back together.

Walk Away

Finally, you should be prepared to walk away. If there is no way around the deadlock and you have tried most of the options above with no success, then this is probably one of those occasions when you are not going to be able to do a deal.

Key Takeaways

It may be that the negotiation is not actually in deadlock, so test it by one or more of the following:

- Restate the issue and listen
- Change the location
- Change the negotiator
- Bring in a mediator/arbitrator/boss
- Point out the consequences to all
- Have an off the record conversation
- Change the package
- Take an adjournment
- Walk away

Further Thought

Deadlock cannot always be resolved. You can spend months or years trying to reach an agreement, but in the end, you may just have to walk away. This can feel like failure, but it will not be as big a failure if you accept a bad deal. If you can put your hand on your heart and say that you have revisited your planning, engaged with others to seek their input, assessed all the options both directly and indirectly associated with the deal and pushed the other side as hard as you could, you can walk away with the confidence that you gave it your best shot, but the deal on the table was beyond your confirmed Red Line.

Environments for Negotiating

The location or method for negotiating can have as big an impact on the outcome as the performance of the individuals or teams, but it is often the least well thought out and can undermine as well as support a position.

I have lost count of the number of times I have been shown into a meeting room, been told to make myself at home as my contact will be with me in a few minutes and quickly found discarded items from the previous meetings. I don't go into rooms looking for this, but it is often harder not to see it. Flip-charts are one of the biggest culprits. How often do you take the paper away after a meeting, or is it just flipped over to show the next fresh clean page? I have found sales targets, client lists and even competitor pricing information.

I held a strategy session with an international supplier at an offsite facility and had to collect 6 copies of their target lists that had been left behind by team members who were distracted by calls and emails as they left.

One final tale of warning comes from social media. One of my clients had a great run of success and wanted to build on it to continue to grow their business. When we looked back at how they identified the last few targets, they told me it came from a photo a friend, who had just had a baby and posted on social media. There were three things in that photo that caught his eye, the baby, the boss and the target list on the whiteboard behind the boss.

This section will look at three main environments for negotiating:

- Face-to-face
- Telephone
- Email

Face-to-Face

As well as the tactics, process and planning, there are two other key elements to consider when preparing for a face-to-face negotiation: where it will be held and how the room will be set up.

Location

When it comes to the location, there are three choices: our office, their office or a neutral venue.

Everybody recognises the analogy of home-field advantage. You are in familiar surroundings, you have all your support staff there, you know the good places to grab a sandwich at lunchtime, and you can control the environment. But there are also significant downsides to being at home. They will get to see how you operate; they also get to see your offices, the cars in the car park and the competitors who are just leaving (because that meeting overran by 25 minutes); they even see the paintings and décor – and they get to act dumb when trying to find the bathroom. So, if you are going to try to take advantage of getting them to come to your office, make sure it does not backfire.

The second option, in terms of preference, is to hold it at a neutral location. This can work well if there is a great distance between both parties or you happen to be in the same location as each other and it is convenient. But you need to work out in advance who is going to pay for the venue – if a room, refreshments or AV is required.

Finally, you could go to their offices. This tends to be the least favoured option because you are travelling out of your comfort zone and you are taking up time. This only gets worse the further you travel. But because we are less comfortable, we are probably more alert and aware of what is going on both in the room and in the wider environment. They are the hosts and how they welcome you will tell you a lot about how they view the potential relationship. There are no distractions for you as all you need to do is turn your phone off. As for being out of your own territory, don't rush things. Give yourself time.

There are advantages and disadvantages to each location. You need to decide which will be best for you on a negotiation-by-negotiation basis.

Room Set-Up

What kind of an atmosphere you are trying to create will very much dictate the environment of the room set-up.

An open, friendly, cooperative environment is best created in an open, bright and airy location, possibly with nice views and plenty of refreshments on hand. If you are planning to play the pauper card, then perhaps having top-of-the-range refreshments served in a stunning boardroom may not be quite as effective as water and coffee in a lower level meeting room.

The physical requirements for each room are very much down to the individual expectations and requirements. If there are going to be detailed drawings used during the negotiation, then some place to lay these out should be made available, or a screen and projector may be required. If you are going to sit around a table, beware of the barrier effect that this can have. Also seating positions around the table can cause conflict both across the table and along the table.

Telephone

What different tactics, if any, can you use in telephone negotiations to increase your likelihood of achieving your goals?

First thing to recognise is that to give yourself the best opportunity, you should initiate the telephone call, either by calling the counterparty or by setting a mutually acceptable time for the call.

If you receive a call out of the blue and are not prepared then you should apologise, tell them now is not a great time and set a time to call back.

So, for telephone negotiations the keys lie in preparation, management, recording and focus.

Preparation

The amount of preparation you put into a telephone negotiation should be no different than preparing for a face-to-face negotiation. You are still going to be having a dialogue with one or more counterparties with the intention of trying to reach an agreement.

Management

Know what is achievable in the time allotted for the call and map this to the five steps, but don't rush any of the steps. The first step, Scene Setting, may go by more quickly than face-to-face, and you may need to do a little more leading to get people to contribute – but it should still be there.

People's attention span is shorter on telephone calls than in a face-to-face meeting. Plan your time with this in mind.

Also, if this is a follow-up phone call, don't assume that the same people are on the call. Always check, as you cannot see who is on the other end of the call.

Recording

Take detailed notes from the call, especially commitments or agreements. Take advantage of the phone environment to note the significant words, phrases, tone and other strategic messages sent and received. In particular, document commitments made by you and/or your counterpart.

Shortly after your conversation, draft an email to confirm those commitments in writing. When you send this email, ask them to let you know if your email does not accurately reflect their understanding of those commitments. You don't want ambiguous commitments or misunderstandings that can lead to problems later.

Focus

Finally, it's so easy to get distracted while on the phone, usually checking and responding to emails or having someone popping his or her head around the door for a quick question. Shut yourself off from all distractions and focus on the call.

Email

Every day, more and more people are turning to email to try to speed up the negotiation process. This creates challenges - – such as ease of use, misinterpretation and relationship building, but can also make it easier to get some form of leverage when compared with face-to-face or over-the-telephone negotiating.

Ease of Use

Make sure that the counterparty is happy to use email at all, never mind negotiate by email. There are still a number of people, admittedly from a slightly older generation, who just don't use email and are unlikely, therefore, to want to negotiate via email. So, make sure that email will work by asking them in advance.

Misinterpretation
There is no tone, visible gesture or smile that goes with an email, so be very careful that what you write is not going to be misread by your counterparty. Also, don't respond in haste. It is very easy to fire off a quick response when we are out and about, distracted, thanks in the main to Blackberry. Take your time, consider carefully what is being said and respond appropriately.

Relationship Building
Because we are essentially talking with a screen, there is no one with whom to build a relationship. That does not mean you cannot be friendly, using emoticons :) or ;) or :D or :| to build an amicable email-based relationship. Because we are committing things in writing, we tend to be more careful about what we say which, while honest, true and factual, can become dry, dull and potentially offensive. So, go easy on the language; be clear and direct, but keep it all conversational.

Leverage
The power of email comes in the ability to ask questions you might not ask if you were face-to-face. You can dig deeper for other areas of common interest and speak to the ego of the person you are negotiating

with. Praise them and, most of all, be humble if you want to get the highest return on your time. You'd be surprised at what you can draw out of a person via email by taking an interest in them. Ask the open, G.R.I.P.-type questions to get them "talking" about themselves.

Key Takeaways

Environments for negotiating:

- The environment is just as important as the content, so plan it carefully.
- Face-to-Face
  - Where are you going to hold it?
  - How will you set up the room?
- Telephone
  - Prepare as if face-to-face.
  - Manage the time carefully as attention spans can be shorter.
  - Record as much as you can, summarise regularly and follow-up quickly.
- Email
  - Are they happy to use the technology?
  - Be careful of misinterpretation. You may write something with a smile on your face, but that smile may not be interpreted by the reader.
  - It is easy to be too short or direct; think about the counterparty style and adapt your emails to fit.
  - Don't ignore the relationship building element; email is not just for facts.

Further Thought

Remember you need to be in control. Which environment will maximise your control?

How Can I Be More Influential?

Robert Cialdini, a Regents' Professor of Psychology at Arizona State University, identified that there are six psychological principles which, if used correctly, can help you to become more influential. These principles are:

1. Reciprocation
2. Consistency
3. Social Proof
4. Liking
5. Authority
6. Scarcity

Individually, they are very powerful, but in combination, they become almost irresistible.

Reciprocation

Cialdini describes this as the "good old give and take." He goes on to say that one of the most potent weapons of influence is the rule of reciprocation. The rule says that we should try to repay, in kind, what another person has done for us.

This is one of the most pervasive rules within society, as studies have shown that all human societies buy into this rule.

What does this mean for the negotiator?

First, you need to be aware of its power and influence so that when someone gives you something (such as a concession) in a negotiation, you don't automatically reciprocate.

Second, when you make a move, it is likely to trigger a similar response.

Thirdly, if you start with a large request which gets turned down, the next, slightly smaller, target request is likely to be accepted because you are seen to have retreated, or made a concession, after the rejection.

Consistency

Leonardo Da Vinci said: "It is easier to resist at the beginning than at the end."

The principle of consistency comes from our desire to appear to be consistent with what we have already done. Once we take a stand, we will feel that we must behave consistently with that stand.

Cialdini says that we simply convince ourselves that we have made the right choice and, no doubt, feel better about our decision.

What does this mean for the negotiator?

Firstly, if we can get the ball rolling by getting the counterparty to make small commitments early on, they may well agree to larger items later in the process out of duty.

Secondly, question every decision you make on its merits. Just because something seemed like a good idea three weeks ago does not mean that something similar is a good idea today.

Social Proof

The basic premise of this principle of influence is that people like to see other people doing something before they do it. We check to see if it is OK to do before we do it. Ever broken the speed limit because everybody else was or left your newspaper on the train because there was a pile on the table or seat when you got on?

Dancing is a great, non-negotiation example of this. Some organisations will pay professional dancers to dance at their parties. Why? Well, no one wants to be the first person onto an empty dance floor, so having others doing it is more likely to get you to do it as well. Throw some uncertainty into the mix and you will strengthen the desire to act with the crowd. If I see that no one else is dancing, then I am not going to and I will probably also convince myself that it is because the song/band/DJ is not very good rather than acknowledging the truth which is that I don't want to be the first to make a move.

What does this mean for the negotiator?

Firstly, it means that if you can demonstrate or persuade the other party that what you are proposing is standard and that everybody else is doing it, there is a much greater chance of them doing it.

Secondly, if you can create an attractive model of behaviour that is replicated by everybody on your side of the table, there is every chance that the other party will start to mirror this behaviour.

Finally, you need to assess your behaviour and actions in context, and if they don't line up then you are probably falling victim to the principle of social proof.

Liking

Three different people are going to ask to borrow £50 to get a taxi home because they have missed the last train. To whom would you be more likely to say yes?

- The person you have never met
- The person you dislike
- Your friend

I think that, for most of us, it would be the friend; this is the principle of liking in action.

Now take this one stage further and our friend is not there. Instead, the third person is a stranger who mentions your friend's name. So, we now have:

- The person you have never met
- The person you dislike
- The person who mentions your friend's name (in a good way)

Once again, we are more likely to help the third person, even though the friend is nowhere to be seen. This is another example of the principle of liking in action.

If we can get people to like us, there is a much better chance they will come under our influence.

What does this mean for the negotiator?
Firstly, try to build a relationship with the other parties; try to get them to like you and/or respect you.

Secondly, dress appropriately and look after your personal hygiene. People don't like scruffy, smelly people.

Finally, recognise when you find yourself starting to like the other party more than is appropriate under the circumstance, and don't let this influence your decision.

Authority

This principle is triggered when your decision is influenced by the real or perceived authority of the other party.

What does this mean for the negotiator?

Firstly, you need to establish your authority within the scope in which you are operating.

Secondly, don't be afraid to bring someone with more expertise along. True authority is often demonstrated by admitting that you don't know everything and that you are not frightened to rely on the knowledge of others.

Finally, always question the truth behind the authority claims. Are they really an expert? Get your expert in. Are they really the most senior person in the team? Check what their job title really means.

Scarcity

People are often more motivated by the thought of losing something than by the thought of gaining something, so while it might seem that it would be good to give something to get things moving, it can be more effective to take something away.

The basic premise behind this principle is that things appear more valuable when they are less available. In other words, if I don't take this now, I might lose it.

What does this mean for the negotiator?

Firstly, time pressure is a real and powerful friend. If you know they want something, then why not put a time limit on it? Tell them they have until Friday.

Secondly, make an offer or go for a close just as a deadline is approaching.

Thirdly, if it is appropriate, make it sound as if what you are offering is a "special" just for them. You don't do this for anybody else, so they will gain an advantage by doing it your way.

Finally, if you reckon that you are being made to feel that something is scarce or that you are being offered something than can be easily taken away, don't accept it. Take your time and assess its merits under your terms.

Key Takeaways

Being more influential:

- There are six keys for influence
  - Reciprocation
  - Consistency
  - Social Proof
  - Liking
  - Authority
  - Scarcity
- Identify which will work best for you in your situation.

Further Thought

Robert Cialdini has written a book that provides much more information behind each of these keys as well as details of the experiments used to prove their existence. The book is called *Influence – The Psychology of Persuasion* and is well worth reading to understand this subject further.

30301871R00107

Printed in Poland
by Amazon Fulfillment
Poland Sp. z o.o., Wrocław